The Lake Bodom Blood Murders

D.Z Matt Demas

(August 2004)

There was an older gentleman who was placed in a chair, sitting at a table with his hands cuffed. He was all alone in the room. The entire room was dark except for where he was placed. Above him was a bright, florescent light that shined down on him like heaven. That was just about the only thing in the dark, cooled room, not counting the table and two chairs. He sat and waited patiently. Although he was not sure of what he was waiting for, he sat patiently.

After a long period of time, the door to the room opened. The older gentleman had not a clue on how much time had passed, but he was curious to see what was to come next. A man entered the room and walk towards the table. It was obvious that he was a policeman, or even a detective. He was casually dressed and his badge was clipped to his belt. He was a younger looking man, who appeared to be in his early 30s and he even wore hair gel, being certain that his hair would not fall out of place. He placed himself at the table with the older gentleman. They just stared into each other for a brief moment. The older gentleman just starred blank. He had no emotion to him what so ever. The man of authority could not make up his mind. He would either smile at him, or stare at him with fury.

The man of authority pulled out a pack of cigarettes and lit one up. He held the pack out, offering a cigarette to his company, but the man didn't budge, so he just placed them on the table in front of him. He took a drag from his cigarette.

"We got you now... Over forty years later, but we got you now." He said calmly, but with win and satisfaction behind his tone of voice.

The older man, still starring into his eyes with no emotion responded with win as well, but also with a hint of shame in his voice.

"What's done is done... I'll get fifteen years."

The young man of authority immediately locked eyes with him. To him it felt as if he just heard a murder confession.

"It doesn't matter to me. I don't think you could live another fifteen years and that still don't matter. What does matter is we got you. Five years, ten years and it still doesn't matter. What we have today that didn't exist then will finally bring justice to the friends you've horrifically murdered at Lake Bodom. Here's a sincere question for a small portion of closure for me. I want to know why you did it. Why did you do it?"

The older man still did not show any emotion and he did not answer the young detective's question.

"It's Okay. You don't have to tell me anything at all. It's not like it will change anything. The evidence that we have against you will show in the end and it'll bring to you what you deserve."

The man of authority stood up from the chair and walked towards the door.

"I'll be right back." He said exiting the room.

He took a walk down the hallway to another room. He opened a file cabinet and ended up going through the case files that held all the information about the Lake Bodom murders. He searched and found the old case files from the murders in 1960. He looked through them fast. After finding the murder pictures he bumped into another man of authority. The man had much higher authority than what he had. He was an older detective who happens to see what the younger man of authority was possessing. After grabbing the case files from his hand and skimming at them he made eye contact with him. He starred at him in a certain, serious way.

"I was twenty years old when that happened. It was a very sad and scary scene."

"You were there?"

"Let me ask you something boy... Do you know what you're doing in there?"

"I think so." He said laughing.

"You can't think so." Said the veteran detective, as he started placing the murder scene pictures on a table, in a line.

"Take a look at these. It is much different looking at the scenes in pictures compared to actually being there. I can still remember like it was yesterday when I first walked on to the scene and witnessed what I saw. A scene like that isn't hard to forget."

The veteran detective got into his story mode of remembering that day in 1960.

"It was a warm, sunny morning when I first got the call. It wasn't long later when I arrived at the murder scene. The first thing I did see was two motorcycles, which belonged to the victims. Not five seconds later did I hear the sounds of grunts and groans... Kind of like a zombie. I walked over to the obvious murder scene, just for me to see a young boy lying over top of his tent. The tent was shredded and covered with blood. As I analyzed the young boy, looking at what happened to him, I could then realize that inside the shredded tent, were three battered and bludgeoned corpses. I can still see the red. The three victims were stabbed to death and beaten with something... Two twenty-two year old girls and two twenty-three year old boys. The one male victim in particular was just beat up horribly bad... A broken jaw, a couple of bruised bones in his face, and a whole lot of cuts and lacerations. It still gives me the chills when I think about it. That was me being introduced to horror."

"But, what about then... You never had any leads? There had to be something."

"We had about a half dozen suspects, who all happen to have solid alibis. There was not one person we could convict... Not one. However, there was one person in particular that stood out to me. He worked a kiosk on the land, selling lemonade to the joggers and campers. The man hated the campers for whatever reason, I don't know. I think it was the younger generation that he hated for some reason. He later ended up drowning himself in the lake. Before he drowned he confessed that he was the Lake Bodom murderer."

"Was it him?"

"We investigated it. His wife said he never left the house and he was home during those times. They thought it out to be a cry for help. Just somebody looking for any kind of attention, but I thought it out to be him. There was another time we thought we had another lead from the group of boys who were bird watching. They were the group who also discovered the murder scene. They said that they saw a man leaving the scene through the wooded area. The man they described leaving the scene did not match the description to any of our suspects."

"Do you think this is our guy? Could he have done it?"

The veteran detective looked at him with a doubt in his mind.

"I don't think we will ever know, and I don't think that reopening the case is going to change anything besides screw with this man's life."

With that being said, it reminded the younger man of authority of what he heard.

"Detective, you just reminded me. He said to me and I quote,

"What's done is done and I'll get fifteen years."

The veteran detective starred back with a smile.

"Well, he is right about one thing. Come on young detective, let's go pay him a visit. Watch me and learn." Said the veteran detective, waiving him down the hallway to the room. They both entered and the veteran detective greeted him and they both placed themselves in a seat at the table, with their suspect.

"Mr. Niles are you comfortable? Do you need a drink, or anything?"

He did not say one word.

"Look Mr. Niles, giving us the silent treatment isn't going to get this over with any time sooner. You have to say something." Stated the veteran detective with a hint of assertiveness.

Mr. Niles starred up and made eye contact with the veteran detective.

"What can I possibly say? It was over forty years ago." He said and still showed no emotion.

"Listen to me Mr. Niles..."

"Byron. Call me Byron. That's enough with the Mr. bullshit."

"Okay, Byron... You are the only person who knows what happened that night. You got to tell me something."

"Not necessarily. Being beaten in the head doesn't help my memory on top of it being forty plus years later."

"You don't remember anything? There are some things you remember about that night."

"Every time I go to think about it I draw a blank. Do you know what it's like to not remember what happened?"

"Byron, you have to try. At least try to remember before your arrival at the lake. What did you do before you made your stay that night? Give me the story. That can help the both of us. I can help you. It isn't me charging you. Try and start with the beginning of the day. Does that help?"

Byron sat quiet once again. Then he began to shed some tears. It was as if he remembered everything before the horrific event. He began to speak about his lover.

"I can tell you something. Boy we were in love." He said laughing as a few tears dripped down his face, landing on the table.

"We were only together a few weeks, but I'll tell you, the feelings I had for her were strong. I would think about Amelia all hours of the day and night. When I did stop thinking about her, It would be when we would meet up together. I loved riding her around on my bike. It was my favorite thing to do with her. I loved the way her arms felt being wrapped around me and with her cheek rested up against my back. It

made me feel like a strong man, riding a
motorcycle with a woman on the back of it.
Not just a woman, but the one I was in love
with"

"What about Seth and Angel? What can
you say about their relationship?"

"They were in love too. Hell, they
were already together pushing two years. We
all did the same thing, the four of us. We
both had bikes and we both had our ladies.
I met Amelia through Angel. Amelia and
Angel were good friends."

"How were your relationships...? Let's
say intimate wise?"

"What? Why is that important?"

"I know it sounds weird, but it lets
me know and helps me develop a picture and
idea of every event that happened that
day."

"We weren't active in sex just yet."

The veteran detective took a brief
moment of mind puzzling.

"Alright. Not just you two though, but the four of you. Was there sexual activity in Seth and Angel's relationship?"

"Seth and Angel were in an in-love, sexual relationship. As for me and Amelia, she was a virgin. It reminds me... We were to lose it to each other that night at the lake."

His mind drifted off for a moment and he began to stare around the room. The veteran detective was repeatedly asking Byron a question, but he was not responding to him. After a loud hammer fist down on to the table, Byron finally came to his attention.

"Did you, or did you not lose your virginity to her that night!" The veteran detective stressed.

Byron starring blank, answered in a very low tone in his voice,

"I don't know... I can't remember."

"It's Okay. Then all we do is move past that and we can come back to it. What else can you tell me?"

"I do remember buying condoms from a merchant on the corner. So it could have happened. We bought booze too."

"Okay. Good Byron. Very well put... What can you tell us about your friendship with Seth? Were you two good pals? Were you two close buddies?"

"We were friends for about ten years give or take. We did shop for bikes together and got them the same day. I can remember us racing each other home." He started laughing in joy.

"So, it sounds like you guys were a pretty, tight clique of friends."

"We were off and on from time to time."

"What do you mean?"

"Well, you know how friends argue. Pretty much like you guys. I'm sure you told officer pretty boy to let you take over and watch how you do things... Right?" Byron said laughing, once more."

Both detectives followed laughing.

"I'm sure you know how the youngsters act in this era. You have to show him the ropes. However, what we are doing right now is just trying to help you. Listen Byron, I saw you at the scene. You were beaten and bloody. I want to help you. Whether you did it or not, I do not really care. You don't have to tell me. You can just let the court, judge, and jury decide. On the second hand, there's a part of me that says you didn't do it. I can be completely up front and honest with you and tell you what I should really keep to myself... Byron, I cannot make myself believe that you are the cold blooded killer. Yes, we all know that the injuries you sustained were not as severe as your dear friends, but you did suffer from severe injuries. We do know that your companion, the woman you were in love with... She was stabbed a dozen times, or more after she was already dead. Yes, there are some serious inquires about whether or not you did it. That is the system though Byron... With my reasonable doubt... My personal, reasonable doubt of opinion. I cannot come to terms and say it was you. Can you remember the lemonade vendor? The man working the kiosk on the land. Tell me about him Byron. Please don't tell me that you don't remember."

"I do remember him." He said in his typical, low unemotional attitude.

It was as if Byron was having mood swings. If he was not laughing at a joyful memory, or shedding tears over a saddened memory, he was without emotion. No sadness, anger, or even a sign of being happy. Byron may not have been mentally healthy. It slowly grew to become a toy to his brain, but it also began to shine memories back to his routine in 1960.

"What do you remember Byron?" The veteran detective asked by yelling and not having the patience to wait for an answer.

"I remember him being a very miserable, rude person. Especially for a guy to sell beverages at the lake where people jog and camp. I think I remember hearing stories about him throwing stones at the campers. That's all I can really say about him."

"Byron try and remember the day. Focus and try to remember the day that all of you first arrived at the lake. You have to try. Try and remember all the way up until you decided to call it the night and go to sleep."

The veteran detective was determined to get Byron to remember and talk.

The veteran detective could taste that he was finally going to know what happened that night. It did not matter to him if it would have put Byron behind bars. He did not care whether or not if he was the killer. It became a matter of just a peace of mind for him, after forty years. Although he believed in justice, he would die to know what happened that night in every minor detail.

"You won't stop asking me to remember will you?" Asked Byron.

"I will not stop asking you, Byron."

"You keep saying my name, but you never even told me yours, detective..."

"Wrighmas. Allen Wrighmas."

"I'll talk to you, but I'll only do it under one circumstance."

"What is your one circumstance?"

"I'm not going to talk, or share anything and I'll stop everything right now and we'll just move forward... I don't want the young egotistic, power-tripped kid with hair gel that thinks he's a detective in my presence. However I will talk to you, Detective Wrighmas."

The both detectives starred at each other.

"You heard the man. Get lost."

"Do I really have to go? You won't talk with me in here?"

"He wants you gone Michael. Now get lost."

Detective Wrighmas escorted him to the door, opening it and then shoving him out. Slamming the door shut, he walked back over and placed himself at the table.

"Please tell me they didn't hand a murder case to a kid like that?" Asked Byron.

Detective Wrighmas started to laugh.

"I like the way you think."

They sat quiet for a brief moment. Byron saw the cigarettes that the young detective left at the table. He reached across and took a cigarette from the pack and lit it, using the lighter. He leaned in and handed the pack over to Detective Wrighmas.

"No thanks, I don't smoke." He said.

"Let me tell you something Allen. I don't like talking about this. It hasn't left my head for forty-four years. It sickens my stomach and I think it's downright arrogant... A flaw in the corrupt system." He said very boldly.

"Don't look at me like I'm the one who made the decision and charged you with three murders. Especially over forty years later." He said, laughing.

"Oh, I definitely know it's out of your hands and way above your head."

"I think it's time we quit the bullshittin' Byron. Let's get down to the bottom. I want to know what happened that night at the lake."

"I will tell you what I can. I cannot promise that everything will be clear, but I'll do my best to tell you what I can remember."

Byron sailed off into his mind and began to speak it out.

July 1960:

Byron and Seth set off on their motorcycles. They had their girlfriends, Amelia and Angel riding along with them on the back. They held their men tight, as they rode freely with speed. They were heading for a joyful night at the beautiful Lake Bodom. They all planned on having a party between the four of them and camping the night out. Upon their arrival at the lake, they picked up a four person tent in Espoo, at a local store.

Upon their arrival at Lake Bodom, they took a short ride down a trail until they came across a satisfying spot to camp and pitch their tent. The spot they ended up finding was at a close distance to the lake, and a big enough spot for their tent and a fire. They retired from their motorcycles. They parked them both in between trees. That is when they searched for a decent spot to pitch their tent.

After a long decision of finding a spot for their tent, it still was not agreeable between the four of them. How their tent was pitched, was not the smartest way to pitch a tent. Their tent was fairly close to the lake. The ground also seemed to be on a slope rather than it being on a level ground.

"I guess that about does it." Seth said.

"Yep. If that's the way you want it." Byron said.

The four of them stood back starring at their tent. None of them seemed to care either way on how their tent was set pitched, being it took them a while to set it up. They were happier to just have it pitched so that they could finally begin their fun time. Byron turned to Amelia.

"Hey hottie, come take a dip in the lake with me." He said with persuasion.

Amelia began laughing.

"Hey! Are we all not invited?" Asked Seth.

"Well, of course you're all invited... I was flirting with my better half. Wasn't I Lia?"

Amelia began laughing again.

"You two are so cute." Angel said, laughing."

"Why are we all standing here? Let's go!" Yelled Seth, as he went sprinting towards the lake.

Byron scooped Amelia up and over his shoulder. He started to run, following

Seth. Angel followed behind them. They all jumped into the lake and began their enjoyment.

They were all having a wonderful time. They were splashing and taking turns dunking each other. They were even swimming under the water and started competing to see who could make-out under the water the longest.

"Hey man, do you know what really sucks?" Byron stated.

"What might that be?" asked Seth.

"It would've been pretty cool if we would've brought some fishing pools."

"Yeah, it would of. The fishing is good down here." Seth said.

"Fishing's boring." Amelia interrupted.

"Fishing is not boring." Byron replied.

"When have we, or do we ever go fishing?" Amelia asked.

Byron stopped to think for a moment. Seth began to laugh at him. Byron and the girls followed.

"You shouldn't have to think about it. We never have gone fishing."

"Okay. You're right about that, but it still isn't boring though."

(Present Time- 2004)

"Just let me jump in and interject real fast... How much time do you think the four of you all spent, swimming in the lake?" Asked Detective Wrighmas.

"I can honestly say it was a good while. It was probably about an hour or 2, give or take. Why? Is that really important?" Answered Byron.

"Not necessarily. It's not highly important, but just for my own knowledge. You can't remember if you saw anybody pass by your site, nor were you in site of your tent while you were in the water?"

"Not a soul... Not- a- soul." Said Byron.

"By the time you all finished swimming in the water, was it dark, or becoming dark at all yet?"

"Nope. It wasn't getting dark yet. It was still daylight for a while and we still did some things before it was getting dark."

(Past Time- 1960)

The companions finished their clowning around and horse play in the lake. They got out and dried themselves off. They decided that before they did anything else, they were just going to relax and hang out at their campsite.

"It definitely would be a good idea if one of you strong survival men got a fire going. That way we can make some food, relax, and drink a little." Angel said, making a joke.

"Do you really want to do a fire already?" Byron asked.

"Yeah, and why not?" Amelia asked, joining in to side with Angel.

"I guess it wouldn't hurt to at least gather up some wood while we still have daylight to see." Seth stated.

"I'm hungry. I want to eat something." Angel said.

"Well, alright. We'll get some wood and I'll build a fire so you can all eat." Seth said, as if it was becoming an aggravation to him.

Both men left their campsite, leaving their ladies to occupy it. They were to gather up a load of wood to build their campfire. As both of them went further into the woods to gather wood with their lazy attitudes, the ladies carried their gossip about them.

"Seth can be so lazy some times. I swear I do everything for him. He would forget everything too if I never reminded him." Angel said, laughing.

"I can't say that about By yet. What I can say is that he's always doing things to make me smile. He asks me if I'm okay a lot."

"But you two are really cute together though. I can tell that you'll be with him for a while... If not forever."

"Do you really think so?"

"Absolutely. Do you not see it? You both connect so well together!"

"What do you mean?" Asked Amelia.

"Lia! How he talks to you, how he looks at you... He does always make sure that you're okay. He always makes sure that he's keeping that smile on your face!" She said, laughing but being serious at the same time.

Amelia began to smile. She started to laugh after she thought about it.

"He does. Doesn't he?"

"Do you feel the same way?" Asked Angel.

"Yeah... I do."

"You say it like you're doubting yourself."

"No way! I do love Byron. I just didn't notice that you were able to tell and can see how much By feels for me."

Further away in the woods where Byron and Seth were gathering wood, they were having their own conversation about their ladies as well.

"Yeah man, don't take it the wrong way at all, I'm just saying that you're lucky. You have a cute, attractive lady and she loves you." Seth retorted to Byron.

"What do you want me to say man? Thank you for thinking that Lia is hot?" Byron said, keeping his patience with a cool attitude.

"Hey man, I never said hot. That word never came out of my mouth. I complimented you and your lady in the most respective manner as possible."

"Yeah man, but some things are best just left unsaid. It can make me feel weird just knowing that my best friend thinks my significant other is hot... This can also mean other things too."

"Man... Come on By. Please don't take it that way at all... Seriously, please don't take it that way? It'll bug me and I'll be the one who's feeling uncomfortable."

"Yeah, but you were the one who brought it up." Said Byron.

"Yeah, I did, but I was being respectful and just letting you know that I'm glad you have something good happening for you and you both are happy together."

"Alright Seth... Let's just forget about it."

"Do you mean that?" Said Seth, with a hint of relief.

"I wouldn't have said it if I didn't."

"Good. I don't want to be a burden on our little vacation we have going on."

Byron burst out laughing. Seth was starring confused and then followed laughing. He had not the slightest clue why they were laughing, but Byron was making him laugh.

"What's so funny?" Seth said, still laughing.

"I had you going man. I was Josh-in' you the whole time." He said, still laughing as well.

"About what?"

"Dude are you kidding me? Do you really think I care that you think Amelia is hot?"

Seth stopped laughing and thought for a moment.

"Alright. You did! You definitely got me. I'm glad you were joking because that was bugging me." Said Seth, with even more relief.

(Present Time- 2004)

"Now, at least be honest with me. Were you really joking with him, or did you say that just to burn out the subject itself?" Asked Detective Wrighmas.

Byron gave somewhat of an embarrassing facial expression.

"It did bother me, and I wasn't really kidding with him. I only said it because I can tell it really bothered him, and it was funny, but I also didn't want it to ruin our "vacation" weekend."

"How did you take it though? Did you believe him, or do you think he was curious of her without her clothes on... Do you know what I'm saying?"

"Well, you know how we all think. If another man tells you that your girlfriend is cute, hot, attractive, or whatever... You know they want to get their clothes off."

"So, that's how you took it then?"

"Are you trying to ask me something else?"

"Byron, if I wanted to ask you if you think your friend wanted to poke your lady friend, I would ask... And for the record, did you?"

Byron giggled for a few seconds.

"Yeah, I think so. That's not hard to figure out."

There was an uncomfortable silence for a brief moment. Detective Wrighmas was beginning to have thoughts spinning in his head like wheels. Byron sat quietly waiting for the next question.

"Uh... Byron just answer this to the best of your ability. Hell, we've all thought it, but do we ever really have the guts and follow through with it? The truth is, you'll never know."

"Get to the point already because I have no idea what you're talking about."

"What's your hurry?"

"Seriously detective?"

"Byron... Would you ever think that it's necessary to kill someone over a girl? In love or not?"

"Boy, this is a tough one."

"Take your time. You have enough."

"You're throwing a lot of digs at me all of a sudden. I would kill someone over a girl if they were hurting her, or trying to kill her. I would never kill another person out of jealousy."

"But why do you think your friend would want to have sex with your girlfriend?"

"I want you to think about it. You know that a guy would stick his garbage in anything they can get their hands on. Especially if they find them attractive."

"Even though that it is your friend?"

"Things happen. Even if it is your friend. It would take a real friend not to pull secrets behind your back... Even with your girlfriend especially and real friends, you don't really ever have."

He grabbed another cigarette and lit it.

"Well said Byron... Well said."

"Do you want me to go back to my story now?"

"Level and fire."

(Past Time-1960)

The four young companions sat around the fire filling their stomachs with food and beer, sharing jokes and having laughs.

"I swear we're like the only ones around out here." Byron stated.

"Except for that lady washing her clothes in the lake." Seth said, pointing between the trees.

They all looked and notice a middle aged lady doing her laundry in the lake just keeping to herself. Spontaneously, Byron had the sudden idea to go on a hike.

"So, what's next on the list? Does anyone want to take a walk?"

"Where are we taking a walk to?" Seth said, making a joke out of it.

"Shut the hell up man... We can hike, is what I'm saying."

"I'll go on a hike with you babe." Amelia said, grabbing hold of Byron's arm.

"Yeah, Seth lets go." Angel Said.

"Let them go. We can hang out here, around the fire."

"Oh... So you want some alone time, do yah?" Amelia said laughing, and then everyone followed.

Byron stood up, helping Amelia by her hand. He helped her stand up from the log they were sitting on.

"Okay, we shall return." Amelia spoke.

"Don't get bit by a tick, or a snake now, okay!" Seth said, joking as he laughed.

"I'd worry more about mosquitoes biting you on the ass." Amelia said laughing.

After a few byes, they were off to their hike through the trails and woods. At this point in time, the sun was already starting to set. The couple held hands and just slowly strolled down a trail in the wooded area. They were scoping the scenes and noticed a rabbit hop off the trail and enter into the woods. They then saw two more do the same thing.

"Wow, there's a lot of rabbits." Byron said.

"I'm liking the butterflies down here. They are really colorful, and there are so many just flying so free!"

They then noticed a deer along the trail with its fawn. The deer just stood still and stared. Byron and Amelia stood still also. They afraid to make any movements. They did not want to scare them away. They could see that the baby deer was feeding, and they watched.

"There's a lot of exciting nature to see. We saw about a half dozen rabbits and now seeing a mommy deer feed the baby deer." Amelia said, with amazement.

"Do you want to keep going and see what else we can find?"

"Yeah! Let's do it." She said, with excitement and enthusiasm.

They grabbed each other's hands again and continued on their hiking stroll, down the shadowed, secluded trail in the woods. They could hear the sound of chirping birds as if there were hundreds that surrounded them. Byron let go of Amelia's hand and wrapped his arm around her shoulders. He started pulling her in more firmly. She rested her head up against his chest and then wrapped her arms around his waist. He kissed the top of her head. She starred up at him. He then came down with a kiss on her forehead. Then followed by a wet kiss on her lips. She smiled at him with the look of romance as if it flickered in her mind.

"This isn't so bad is it?" Asked Byron.

"No, it's not. It feels good to escape the real world for once. You know what I mean?"

"Definitely. It's not too often that we had many chances to hang out. I'm glad that we do."

"Me too. I'm having a good time with you right now. I am enjoying every second of it." Amelia said smiling,

"So, is there going to be more of us after this?" She asked.

"Inevitably... How about as much as we can? Every day..."

Something caught their attention, and they immediately stopped dead in their footsteps. "Wow! That is so beautiful!" Amelia yelled, being stunned.

They both stopped to admire a beautiful, natural setting of a waterfall. It settled near a creek, and you could not see where the water was flowing from. It fell from a gigantic boulder and had a 7 foot drop into the creek. It was not large water setting, but sizable enough to just be right for where it was homed. It was also enough to amaze Amelia and to give her more of a romantic mood. They both shared the moment and that is when they gave each other a firm kiss. In the midst of their true, romantic moment and kiss, they were startled by the presence of another person. From nowhere came a tall, large mysterious man. Byron greeted the mysterious man, but he was ignored. The man was dressed wearing a purple shirt and dark blue jeans. He was also wearing a pair of black gloves. His hair was short and brown, along with the goatee he let grow on his chin. The facial expression he wore was no ordinary look. It was more like an expression of worry and hurry. They both watched him and greeted him on his pass by, but the man stayed silent and continued his way through. As soon as the man grew out of site that is when Byron and Amelia started their gossiping about the strange man they had just encountered, and the man who just ruined a perfect, romantic moment.

"Who the hell was that guy?" Byron said, laughing.

"Only God knows, but that guy's making me nervous. What is he doing down here all by himself?"

"God only knows that one too. He is one suspicious character. Byron stated, growing a bit curious with a hint of being nervous."

"Do you think he's going to walk past our campsite?" Amelia asked, becoming nervous too and not hiding it.

Byron grabbed Amelia by her sides and kissed her once more.

"Lia relax. Don't over think too much. I'm more annoyed by the disturbance, and besides, I won't let anything happen to you."

"I know you wouldn't... And I wouldn't let anything ever happen to you."

"But I have to be your hero. I cannot let my lovely lady save and protect me. It

has to be the other way around." Byron
said, adding humor to his statement.

 "It doesn't have to be like that all
the time. The woman can save the man too."
"Then the man wouldn't be a man. It is a
man's duty as a man, to protect his better
half at all costs. The woman can't save the
man, period. It cannot happen." He said
once more, becoming debatable."

 "Alright, you can be my hero..."

 "Good... I'm glad I can be." He said,
joking followed by the both of them
laughing."

(Present Time- 2004)

 "So, then you did see somebody else
there at the lake?"

 "One time, and one time only."

 "One time?"

"Yeah. One time. He passed by us, and that was the last we saw of him."

"Only one time?"

"Yes, only one time! Christ, do you understand me now?"

Byron yelled. Detective Wrighmas ignoring the assertiveness continued on past it.

"You said he acted a particular way. Can you tell me in what kind of way was that?"

"I don't know. It was strange. He looked somewhat nervous. He seemed more focused on getting where he wanted to be, or even away from where ever he was coming from. It was strange to me. Even more strange being I never saw him after that."

"Did your friends see him? Detective Wrighmas said quickly, jumping forward too fast."

"I was getting to that. Yeah, they did see him."

"Did they sense anything strange about him?"

"Same thing pretty much. Damn, you ask questions too fast. You want me to talk, and you nail me with questions. It would save you a lot of questions if you would just let me tell you what you wanted to know in the first place."

"Nice speech Byron, but I ask these questions to fill in any potholes. You have to understand that."

"I see. Now, do we want to move forward yet, or do you still want to fill in some potholes?"

"Let's do that Byron. Let's move forward. If I have any more questions, I'll just ask."

(Past Time- 1960)

Byron and Amelia came back to their camp site, entering in the middle of a conversation that Seth and Angel were having.

"Hey, I'm glad you guys are okay!" Exclaimed Angel.

"Why wouldn't we be okay?" Asked Byron.

"Just not even five minutes ago, some really strange guy came past. He even came over and talked to us... Very weird."

"Really? What did he say?"

"Not too much. He walked over and stood by the fire. He just said, it's a good day for fishing and walked away. That's all he said, and that was very random." She said giggling.

"Yeah, he was a strange guy." Seth replied.

"What's even more strange is that we saw him too. He didn't say anything to us though. We said hi and he just kept walking." Amelia said.

"I wonder what he's doing down here by himself." Byron said.

"Who gives a shit about him? I'm ready to go back to drinking." Seth said, becoming anxious.

He stood up from the log he was sitting on and grabbed himself a beer.

"Yeah really, what the hell? Let's do it!" Yelled Amelia becoming anxious as well.

"Listen to you little, party girl." Byron said, joking to Amelia and laughing.

The four companions all adjoined and started the beginning to their partying once again. Seth scooped Angel up and over his shoulder, still holding his beer and not spilling a drop. He began to walk away from their site.

"Seth, what are you doing?" She asked laughing.

"You'll know in a minute. Hey, we'll be right back." He said as he turned his body back to see them.

Angel's body just hung over his shoulder and swayed limp back and forth.

"You all play it safe now. Don't let any strange man ruin your moment and startle the hell out of you." Byron said, making a joke as he and Amelia laughed.

They were already further down the trail and did not respond to Byron's humorous statement. Byron and Amelia placed themselves on a log by the campfire. They were both still laughing at Seth and Angel.

"I definitely know where they're going." Byron said.

"Oh, do you? Is that right?" Amelia said, in a secret, flirting way.

"Well, yeah. Don't you?"

"I don't know if we're on the same page. I could be thinking something totally different."

"You can tell me... Or maybe show me."

"Is that right?"

"Absolutely."

Byron grabbed hold of Amelia and began kissing her. As she gripped on to him,

Byron lifted her from the log and carried her to the inside of the tent. Once they were inside of the tent, they continued their kissing, but now they were becoming extremely aggressive. Their hot romance stepped to a further level of the experimental roughness of the romance. Amelia ripped Byron's shirt from him and began to undo his pants. Byron followed, moving with the gentle kisses to her neck. He moved his hand up her body with a slow gesture, moving past her face and brushed his fingers through her hair. Away from the campsite, Seth and Angel stumbled across a clearing deep in the woods. This was their comfortable spot to start their passionate, love activities together. Seth and Angel never fell out of love and never once did their feelings get sour. They also had more of a kinky, rough side in their love making relationship. Their feelings were deep and strong for each other, and they were always willing to do anything from one to another. They were also a spontaneous couple. They stayed happy, and they stayed keeping each other happy. They were a couple who could grow old together. Back at the campsite with Byron and Amelia, they lay next to each other and were cuddling.

"I love you." Byron said, coming out of the blue.

"Byron, I love you. For a while now I have loved you."

"My feelings for you started to grow after our first night out. I have been wanting to tell you, but I didn't want to move to fast and frighten you off."

"You wouldn't have. The important thing now is I know I'm in love with you."

"And I'm in love with you."

Deep in the woods lay Seth and Angel in their clearing on the ground. They always had a victorious talk with each other after their loving events.

"That was good. You did really good my Angel... We should get it in because it'll be hard to do it in the tent tonight." Seth said.

"You do know how to hit that spot on me. You know how to keep the rhythm going.

Tonight we'll just have to keep sneaking off..."

"We might as well just camp it here. We'll be gone all night... Speaking of which, something just crossed my mind." "What is it?"

"It makes me wonder what they're doing."

"Oh just leave them alone." She said laughing.

"Man. He better be back there doing it."

"Why do you care so much?"

"I don't. I'm just saying."

"Just saying what? Why do you care?"

"It's not that I care... It's just I thought he would have made a move by now."

"Don't worry about them, Seth. They love each other and leave them alone."

"Okay, we can stop talking about it now."

"Well, are we heading back to the campsite now? We probably should." "Yeah... Same place in a little bit, alright?"

"Definitely. I'm in charge next round."

"You don't have to tell me twice."

Back at the campsite Byron and Amelia were still cuddling with each other. Without their knowledge Seth and Angel were making their way to the campsite. Byron and Amelia were speaking about their intimate experience.

"Yeah that did... That felt damn good!" Amelia said, laughing hysterically.

"Yes it did... Yes it did."

"Do you want to do it again?"

"What if they come back?"

"Oh shit that's right! We better hurry up now."

"Rain check definitely."

Once they were dressed and left the tent, they realized that they had company. Seth and Angel stood about 30 feet from the tent and were laughing hysterically as they watched them come out of the tent.

"Are you serious? How long were you two standing there?" Byron yelled.

"Long enough to hear you say, yes it did!" Seth burst out laughing once more.

"Don't forget, do you want to do it again?" Angel joined in.

"Screw the both of you!" Byron yelled, but began laughing as well.

He was able to find the humor in what had just happened.

"That is freaking embarrassing!" Amelia screamed as she stormed away to the trail.

"Hun! Where you going?" Yelled Byron.

"Away from here!" She yelled back.

As Byron went to chase after her, Angel stopped him.

"Relax... I'll go and get her. I can calm her down." She said as she jogged in Amelia's direction.

"We were just joking By. We didn't mean anything."

"I know man it's alright. I thought it was funny too."

"Dude, it was funny." He said, laughing once again.

Byron joined in laughing again.

"Don't wear it out." Byron said.

"You don't have to worry about that because it's going to be funny for a long time."

"Just whatever you do, keep it to yourself. Don't be joking, or laughing about it around Lia. She'll just be pissed off the whole time we're here."

"Don't worry man, I won't. She was the only one to get mad though. I wonder why?"

"I sure as hell don't know why. I think she'll calm down in a minute. In the meantime, I'll have another drink."

"I think I may join you."

They both walked to the cooler, and each grabbed a beer.

"I do have to say man, I was having a good time up until that little misshapen."

"Well, there's no reason to stop having a good time man. You said it yourself, she'll calm down."

Seth picked up a few pieces of wood and placed them inside of the fire. Byron took a seat on the log.

"I wonder how long it'll take for her to come back."

"Not long, man. Chill out."

Further away from their campsite, Amelia and Angel were walking the dark, wooded path. Angel was calming her down along with a mixed conversation.

"It was embarrassing for me. I'm not like you Angel, that stuff is a bit more private to me."

"I know. They're both sorry too. By wanted to come, but I said I wanted to."

"I just don't want it to be talked about anymore ."

"It won't and you can count on that."

"Do you want to walk the path for a little bit?"

"Sure, I don't care."

"You know what I just thought of?"

"What's that?"

"Remember that guy earlier?"

"Shit, how could I forget him?"

"Do you think he has a site set up with other people? I can't see why he would be down here by himself."

"Well, people do come down here, so you have to think about that. He was a bit different though."

"Yeah he was. He freaked me out and got me nervous."

"Okay, I have a question for you."

"I may have an answer."

"What do you think of Seth?"

"What do I think of Seth? Like... You have to be more precise."

"Do you think I have a good guy?"

"Oh, that's what you mean. I like Seth. He can be funny, and I can tell he loves you." "You really think so?"

"Yeah, I do. Why? Do you question your feelings, or relationship with him?"

"I do sometimes. I actually feel weird saying this to you, but your my best friend, so I will tell you."

"Geez, it sounds so serious."

"I sometimes think Seth likes you."

"What!"

"Yes. Please don't say anything?"

"I won't."

"It's the way he looks at you, and
I've seen him checking you out before."

"Angel, you might be being a bit
drastic."

"No, Lia. I am serious. What do you
think?"

"I never really paid any attention,
but you need to talk to him if things are
bothering you."

"I don't know how to go to him. He
might blow it up."

"If you love him, you have to talk to
him. If he loves you, he will listen."

Angel thought to herself and then
agreed with Amelia.

"You're right."

"Don't do it tonight though. We're all
supposed to be having fun so just wait
until tomorrow. At least another day. Do
you want to go back now?"

"Do you? You're the one who left."

"Yeah, let's go back."

(Present Time- 2004)

"So, you boys were getting a bit lucky that night..." Detective Wrighmas said.

"Yeah. You can say that."

"Did you do it more than once?"

"Me and Lia might have done it one, or two more times. We didn't get all sex crazy. As for Seth and Angel. They were like nymphs."

"Really, that bad?"

"They were really into it..."

"From what you tell me... With Amelia becoming embarrassed and upset, it sounds like the normal lady to me. It's good that she wanted to keep herself private."

"That's one thing that attracted me to her. She was a cute lady, and I knew she wasn't a whore. Although, I always asked myself if she could be a trusty, loyal lady."

"Well, was she?"

Byron became silent for a moment and just stared around. Detective Wrighmas remained silent and patiently waited for his answer.

"It's too early to tell."

"It's too early to tell? Why?"

"Was... It was too early to tell. Amelia did come to me and talked to me about a conversation she had with Angel on their walk on the trail. Which to me seemed kind of a similar feeling I had about Seth?"

(Past Time- 1960)

Byron and Seth continued their drinking around the fire. They were laughing about old times and sharing stories. The ladies did not yet make it back to the campsite. Byron and Seth still waited and just continued their conversation about past times.

"You didn't lose your virginity until after high school, right?" Byron asked.

"Yeah... And you're the only one I told that too. You can't say, or tell anybody about that. Angel thinks she's the only one I've been with by the way." "Are you kidding me?"

"No, I'm serious. I'm being honest."

"Well, first thing is first man... Who gives a shit about how many people know that! That's not essential. And second, why the hell did you tell her that?" "I don't know man. I really liked her, and she told me she was a virgin. If I told her the truth then she would have thought I was a pig. I didn't want to screw up any chances with her."

"Angel was a virgin?"

"Yeah. Why do you sound so surprised?"

Byron chuckled a bit.

"I'm not surprised. I was just asking."

"Speaking of the hers... Where the hell have they been?"

"That's a really good question. It's been a bit long since they've left."

"Yeah. It had to be at least an hour. I'm starting to wonder if we should go and look for them now."

"Yeah, but if we leave to go and look for them, then they'll come back while we're gone. Then what?"

"I don't think that would happen. We should run right into them."

"Yeah, I guess so. Do you really want to go and look for them?"

"Yeah, I think we should."

Byron and Seth left their site. They were going to try and catch up with Angel and Amelia so far down the trail.

"I wonder how far they walked. We should probably run into them pretty soon." Seth said.

The traveled a bit far. Once they were a farther distance down the trail and continued to further their travel, they saw that they were not running into them anywhere. The distance that they have traveled should have brought themselves to a meeting somewhere along the way.

"I don't know man. I hope we didn't pass them up somehow. How many other trails are there?" Seth asked.

"All that I know is that it's getting dark pretty soon. We should go back to the campsite before it does."

" Just in case they are there let's just turn around now."

"I told you that it would happen man."

"We don't know that for sure yet...
Let's turn around and go back."

"Are your for certain that that's what
you want to do?"

"Yeah, I'm damn sure. I think we went
far enough. We should have ran into them by
now."

They turned around and started back
towards their campsite. At this point in
time, they were walking much more faster.
Seth's mind was racing, and he was
beginning to overwhelm himself. He was
beginning to think that something had
happen to them.

"Man, they better be there." Seth
said, growing nervous.

"They'll be there man. Don't worry so
much."

"You don't know that. What was taking
them so long? There was that weird guy down
here. We don't know where they are. We
could have past them up somewhere and have
not even of known it because their laying
there dying."

"I'm telling you Seth, you're blowing this up too much. Listen to yourself! Are you hearing what you're saying!" Byron screamed at him.

"I heard what I said. I'll be the one to tell you that I'm blowing it up too much when we get back to the site and see our ladies sitting there by the fire."

"Trust me. They're there man. Don't you worry about that. You're just being a bit dramatic that's all."

"How the hell can you be so calm right now? Our ladies could be anywhere. They can be laying somewhere, bleeding out, dying, and we don't even know where they are?"

"You are too damn dramatic. Relax. When we get back to our site, and they're not there, then start worrying. Don't just jump into being stressed and thinking of the worst when there are still options. You have to quit thinking so negative all the time."

"I just think it's weird that's all."

"Seth! For Christ sake! They're at the God, forsaken campsite! Now, just relax and chill the hell out! If they're not there, then we can start to worry. Okay?"

"Okay. I hope you're as certain as you're making yourself to be. If they're not there, all my anger is getting let out on to you."

"That's fine. I'm sure man. They will be there, and then we'll all be fine. We can start having fun all again."

In under 10 minutes, the sky darkened more with another shade casting over it. The sun was no longer visible, and the night was setting in. From the distance, they were able to see the shining from their fire. The fire was at a widespread. It was able to light up some of the darkened areas around their campsite. This was the only light becoming available.

"It looks like the fire is being tended... Seth." Byron said, with the knowing of him being right.

"Yeah, it is... Yes, you're right and I'm relieved."

They started to walk a bit more faster. As they were approaching their site, they could see figures of two people occupying the site.

"I think I see our ladies Seth. They're not laying and bleeding out anywhere after all." Byron said, laughing and joking with Seth.

"You're real funny By. Do you know that?"

As they came on to the grounds of their campsite, they saw Amelia and Angel sitting on the logs. They were having drinks.

"I told you! You paranoid, pain in the ass!"

"What?" Asked Angel, being curious."

"What! What! Where the hell did you two go?" Seth screamed, being upset.

"We walked the trail and came back."

"We went looking for you because we got worried! How did you two make it back here without running into us?" Byron asked, being over curious.

"There's another trail that meets in the middle. We walked that way." Amelia said.

"Then that explains it. Angel you had me worried. With you taking so long, it being dark and that weirdo down here... I don't know what to expect."

Angel stood up. She walked over to Seth and began hugging him like there was no tomorrow.

"I'm sorry... I didn't mean to make you worry like that."

"It's Okay. I have you back now. I know you aren't lying dead anywhere." He said, laughing.

"Okay! Now that we're all together again, and we're being one big happy family, can we get back to the reason why we came here?" Byron said, laughing.

"That's a good idea. Let's get back in action." Seth said.

"Back in action?" Amelia asked, making a joke as she sipped her drink.

"That's what I was thinking. They were gone, and we were here drinking. We've been in action. You guys have to get back in action. Not us." Angel said as she burst out laughing.

They resumed with their night of fun times and drinks. The companions carried on with their laughs and jokes. It was nothing but good fun for them. It was as if it was only the four of them on their own small island and nothing else existed. They were the happiest two couples in the entire world.

(Present Time- 2004)

"So you think your buddy was over reacting during that whole entire situation?"

"I think he was... Yeah."

"You didn't get nervous at all? Not once? Even with seeing that weirdo lurking about?"

"I did wonder what was taking them so long. I got more curious when we didn't run into them on the trail, but I knew we missed them. Things happen like that all the time and Seth has a habit of being dramatic. If they weren't going to be at our campsite, which is when I was going to become concerned."

"Can you remember what time it got dark down there?"

"I didn't keep track of time while we were down there, really. I would give a rough time, but I'm not certain at all. Is it relevant?"

"I'm just trying to get an idea of when you all stayed at your site for the night."

"It was just becoming dark when we were all back for good. I can remember that much because of the person who was throwing rocks at us."

"So the lemonade man threw stones at you too? Why didn't you tell me that when I first asked you about it?"

"I didn't really plan on talking. I didn't plan on getting this open with you either. I'm keeping you on ice."

"I don't know why you would want to withhold information. This can be a significant help for you with your case. You shouldn't have kept that to yourself."

"I didn't. I just told you. We couldn't really make out whom it was anyway . It was dark, and we were drunk. Whoever it was... They took off on a bicycle, and we weren't chasing after them for that long. It frightened the ladies, and they were wanting to leave after that. We were too drunk to drive out of there, and we figured it was just some dumb kids. So we just did whatever we could do to calm the ladies down. Then we just continued on with our night. Then I think we went into the tent for the night, not long after that."

"So not when just one murder happens, but three murders happen and one survivor who's in critical condition. There was somebody who was attacking them with stones on the night prior to the murders. Yes... It's very important and relevant to your case."

"Well now you have some of the leads now. So it shouldn't really be too late to use."

"It will definitely be used, and you'll have to state that at your trial."

"Wait. Isn't that what the attorneys are used for... A bunch of vampires."

Detective Wrighmas looked into Byron with all strictness.

"You're going to need an attorney for something like this... It's a triple murder case. You cannot go before a judge without an attorney, especially on a triple murder case... That would be heinous. You would be the most stupidest guy on earth."

"I'll do with what I get..."

"What do you say, we get back on track?"

"We can continue the story if you'd
like."

"I'd more than like that Byron...
Enlighten me with your story."

Byron took another cigarette from the
pack and lit it with the lighter. He took a
couple of drags and then resumed back to
his story.

(Past Time- 1960)

The 4 companions, once again adjoined
around the campfire, sharing stories and
telling jokes. Each of them had a drink in
their hand and they were having a good time
laughing. The sky finally settled its
darkest point, and the night was still only
young. Their night was full of unlimited
possibilities. It was dark, and they had a
blazing fire. They pressed on with their
beer drinking and continued to have their
fun without a care in the world.

"Do you know what just crossed my mind?" Seth said, slurring on his words as he staggered around."

"Tell us Seth. What just crossed your mind?" Angel said, laughing.

"Are there other campers? Where are all the other campers? We are seriously the only ones in this spot camping right now. At least on this side that we know of. There was Nobody else who came past here in a car, or nothing. Except that one weird guy."

"I was thinking that earlier. That one guy just came out of nowhere. He never came past again. Unless there's other campers on the other side of the lake, he's gone."

"I think you guys are thinking way too far into it." Amelia said.

"Sounds familiar doesn't it By?"

"Shut up dude. You are the one who keeps bringing up the subject." He said, laughing.

"I'm starting to get tired all of a sudden." Angel stated as she yawned and stretched her arms above her head.

"I hear you. I'm starting to get sleepy too." Amelia replied.

"You can't go to bed yet. The night is still young" Byron said.

"I didn't say I was going to bed yet. I said I was starting to get sleepy."

"I might." Angel said."

"No. You can't go to bed yet either. We're supposed to be having fun. How can we have fun if you two are going to bed?"

"I don't know how much longer I can stay up."

From out of nowhere, Seth was hit in the head by a flying object,

"Ow! Son of a bitch!" He yelled as he stood up. Holding his forehead.

"Are you Okay man? What the hell was that?" Byron said, following Seth standing up.

From nowhere, once more Seth was struck with a flying object and more continued to fly, hitting Byron in the head also. Byron stumbled and fell over the log. Angel and Amelia were ducked down to the ground, dodging them. Byron stood up from the ground after recovering from being hit in the head. When he got to his feet, he was hit once more in the head. He saw where it landed, and he reached down and picked it up. After looking at the object, he discovered that rocks were being thrown at them.

"What the hell man! They're throwing rocks at us!"

Seth was able to pick out the person who was throwing the rocks.

"It's somebody on a bicycle!" Yelled Seth, as he picked up the fire poker and ran after the aggressor.

Byron quickly ran with Seth, following with him. Only running a short distance, they stopped because their attacker was long gone. As soon as they were in route to retaliate, whoever the attacker was, flew

out of there. Byron and Seth were both
stopped. They were catching their breath
and trying to recuperate from the sudden
running.

"What the hell was that all about?"
Byron yelled.

"I don't know man! Go find him and ask
him."

"Yeah real fucking funny, Seth! Now
isn't the time to be a smart ass."

"I'm sorry By. I was hit in the damn
head with a rock... Twice!"

"Seriously man, I'd really like to
know what the hell that was all about."

They took their time and strolled back
over to their site as they recovered from
the fast running and being hit with rocks.

"That was horse shit, Seth. That
really has my mind in the red mode."

"Let it blow over. They might
come back, and we'll definitely grab
hold of him and stick his head in the
fire."

As they came back on to their campsite, the ladies were shook up. They were nervous and frightened after what just happened. They both went into their man's arms for comfort and Byron and Seth, did their part of calming them down.

"It's fine now. It was just some punk ass kids throwing rocks." Seth said.

"I think it's time to leave." Amelia said, being assertive and nervous at the same time.

"Yeah Seth. It's time to go home." Angel replied, in the same mood and attitude.

"We don't have to leave. It was some nerds on bicycles. Let's not let some childish prank ruin our fun night." Byron said, standing his ground while trying to persuade Amelia into wanting to stay.

"How do you know they aren't going to come back?" Amelia asked.

"If they come back, they're not getting away this time." Byron stated, sounding like a tough guy.

"I guess that would answer our questions about other campers being here." Seth said.

"They might not even be campers though. Maybe they were just bicycling." Amelia stated.

"What if it was that weirdo?" Angel asked.

"I think that guy was a bit too big to be on a bicycle. That was just some nerdy kid being a kid." Byron said.

"How certain are you that it was a kid, or even kids?" Amelia asked.

"Who else rides around on bicycles and throws rocks at people? Kids!" Byron said, becoming aggravated.

"Let's all just relax now. Let's just sit back down around the fire and have our drinks. It was some dumb bullshit, and we're Okay. Don't let it ruin your whole night. Seth stressed."

"Well I think I'm definitely going to bed now." Amelia said.

"Why are you going to bed?"

"Because I'm irritated now and I want to go home. So now I'm just going to bed.

"Come on Lia, don't go to bed. I'm going to be upset now."

"We should just go home. I don't feel comfortable and what if they come back while we're asleep and do worse?"

"You're over reacting honey. Just come sit with me and hold my hand."

"I want to go home. Something tells me that they'll come back and do worse."

"If they come back they're getting their asses kicked. Like I said, you're over reacting and you're letting children ruin our moods."

"Do you know for sure? Did you see them?"

Byron and Seth were quiet.

"Well it was dark, but we saw good enough to know it was kids. Kids only do those things.

"Can we please go home?"

Byron looked at Seth. He could tell Seth was not going to leave. He looked at Angel and could tell that she was going to side with Amelia. Byron did not want to leave.

"No, we're not going home. Not now and plus, we've been drinking. Baby just relax. You're blowing this way out of proportion."

"I'm not over reacting, I'm not over thinking, and I'm not blowing anything out of proportion. I want to go home! Amelia said, growing angry.

"We been drinking, and it's dark. We can't go home... Not now."

"Then I'm going to bed By... Good night." Amelia turned away and went inside of the tent.

"I am going too." Angel said as she followed Amelia.

"Come on... Are you really going to bed too?" Seth asked.

"I'm really going to bed Seth."

"Why are you going? Are you mad and wanting to go home too?"

"I'm not mad at you, but going home is a good idea."

"We cannot drive our bikes, and we cannot go home! We've been drinking, what can't you women understand?"

"I think what happened, makes an exception and it's not like you're all drunk. You are both capable of taking us home."

"I'm not taking the chance... It's a gamble. You won't be the one getting a D.U.I, losing your motorcycle and going to jail. We have to stay. It's not an option."

"Fine Seth. I'm going to bed with Lia, and I'll see you in the morning. I love you and goodnight."

"I love you and thanks for not being mad at me."

"See you in the morning." Angel said, retiring into the camp for the remainder of the night.

Byron and Seth just sat on the log, by the fire, drinking their beer. They were quiet. None of them spoke a word when the ladies went into the tent to sleep.

"Well, alright! Seth, you better not be going to bed." Byron yelled, to break the silence.

"I'm not going to bed." He stated like it was the last thing he was going to do.

"I'm not going to bed either, Seth." Byron joked and laughed.

"I know you're not. We're going to stay up for a little bit."

"For a little bit? I might just stay up all night."

From out of nowhere, the ladies came out of the tent and walked over, both sitting on their man's lap.

"We both agreed that we should have gave our gentlemen a kiss good night." Angel said.

"That's very nice of you to think of us like that. It would be even better if you still accompanied us by the fire." Byron said.

"We only came out to kiss you good night. We're not staying up. We are going to bed." Amelia said.

They kissed their better halves good night and retired back into the tent for the night. Byron and Seth, still remained at the campfire, drinking. They were quiet for a brief moment once more, but then started back into conversation all over again. Byron started out by laughing hysterically.

"What's so funny?"

"That was pretty random man. From out of nowhere some asshole just starts throwing rocks at us."

"That was right after we talked about nobody else being close by, or around. What a coincidence that was. If I wasn't so drunk, I would have caught who ever that was."

"In the morning, if we see anybody on a bike we should wreck the hell out of them."

"I'm all for it man."

"One thing I do have to say man is that I had a fun time tonight. I haven't had a chance to do anything like this for a long time. What about you man?"

"I enjoyed myself up until some freak started throwing rocks at us."

Byron laughed once more.

"I know it wasn't funny when it was happening, but it's funny now. Just because how it all happened."

"Yeah... I think we'll have to do this again. We should make this an every week kind of thing."

"Definitely man. It's relaxing, and it's away from the real world. I highly doubt that the ladies would be up for doing this every week."

"I know. Especially after tonight, they'll never want to go camping again at all."

"We'll have to tell them that it's just our thing."

"You know they'd be getting mad. They'd say, why can't we all do something's together? Why does it have to be just you guys?"

They both started to laugh.

"That can be their girl's night out."

"I'll tell you what man, I have to piss like all hell."

"What the hell are you telling me for? Go take your piss."

Byron stood up and walked away from the campsite. He stepped out of the light from the fire for more privacy. He went to a tree and began to do his thing.

Seth was left by himself at the fire. He waited for Byron to finish urinating and continued to drink his beer. He heard the sound of feet trampling on the twigs and dead leaves that covered the ground. He then saw a shadow cast by him. He looked up and saw a figure of a man. He could not make out any features, but he could see that somebody was standing there, and it was not Byron.

"Who the fuck are you?" Seth said, becoming nervous.

The person did not answer. Seth still not able to see clearly, suddenly he was struck across his head with extreme force. The force from whatever object struck him in the head was enough to make him fall over to the ground. Seth could not get back up. He was struck so hard, he could not quite get himself to move. He just lay limp and could not move his legs, or arms. Although he was still conscious he still could not get himself to fully function his body.

As Seth lay on the ground, the unknown person began to rain down stabs to his chest, repeatedly. Seth could only lay there as this person stabbed him over and over again. From nowhere, Byron came into the scene and came to save Seth from the treacherous attack.

"Leave him alone! What are you doing!" Byron screamed at the top of his lungs as he tried to keep a grip on the unknown party and take him to the ground. However the unknown party managed to break free. He struck Byron with the object, causing Byron to fall to the ground. Byron attempted to get up, but was struck once more and even harder. This blow knocked him unconscious. Byron did not move a muscle.

The unknown party took time in stabbing Byron as well. Then from nowhere, a loud scream echoed through the woods. It was Amelia, and she just witnessed her lover being stabbed. She suddenly sprinted out of the tent and began to run for her life as fast as she could. Amelia was hysterical. She was crying the whole time she was running, and when she could, she

would let out a loud, horrific scream. She
had no direction. She was in complete
denial of what she just saw before her
eyes.

She was beginning to become winded.
She could not breathe anymore. She was
exhausted. She was slowing down her pace
and then to the point to where she was
walking. She was sobbing.

"Byron... Byron. Oh my God what
happen... God what happen... What happen?"
She cried.

From out of the blue, at the blink of
an eye, she was gripped by her hair and
then she instantly started to be viciously
dragged back from the direction she was
running. She once again began to scream
hysterically at the top of her lungs.
Amelia began to desperately pray to
herself. She was only waiting to die, but
she could only think of how it was all
going to end. The thoughts that came into
her mind were thoughts such as,

"Is he going to kill me slow, or
torture me... What is his plan and why is

he doing this to us? What did we do to him?
Am I going to be raped and murdered... Or
just murdered? Is there any way I can get
out of this?"

Amelia got the sudden urge to start
screaming as loud as she could once more.
She was hoping that there were going to be
any nearby campers. She also began to think
about Angel, and if she was okay. Amelia
attempted to break free, but it was hard
being that she was getting dragged by her
hair. She even attempted to feel around on
the ground for any type of object that she
could use as a weapon.

"Help! Help! Somebody help me! Let me
go! Let me go!" She screamed, losing her
voice.

She ended up getting her head whipped
back, causing it to slam off the ground.
Her head hit the ground hard. Her forehead
instantly split open. She then began to
get beat with a blunt object all over her
body. She was struck in the head several
times and numerous times on her body. By
the time the unknown party was done beating

her, Amelia lay unconscious and bleeding
out of her head. It did not stop there. The
unknown party then began to stab her
countless times all over her body once
more. Amelia lay and was being abused and
stabbed. Although Amelia already had given
up the ghost, her corpse still lay being
stabbed series after series, over and over
again.

After the unknown party was finished
with their putting to death, they started
to drag her once again, but this time more
aggressive as she was being taken towards
their campsite. Her corpse was being
heedlessly dragged through the wooded area,
hitting off trees and rocks.

At the campsite, Angel hurtled in a
corner of the tent frantically crying. She
was afraid to move. She had not a clue on
what happened. All she knew was waking up
to the sound of Amelia screaming and
knowing her friends were gone. In the
distance, she could hear the sound of
something moving in the woods. She could
hear footsteps stomping on twigs and
sticks. She began to grow frantic even

more. The noises were gaining at a closer distance as if whoever was out there was coming for her. She began to break her silence by crying and whimpering. She could not stay quiet any longer.

Suddenly the noise stopped. Angel could only hear the sound of breathing coming from outside of the tent. She kept her hands over her mouth, trying to keep herself from screaming. Just as she was able to keep herself quiet, Amelia's bloody and abused corpse was tossed inside of the tent. Her corpse landed right next to her. She instantly screamed hysterically at the top of her lungs. As she continued to scream, Seth's corpse was pushed into the tent as well.

Angel was now trapped inside of the tent with her dead lover and dead friend, with a murderer outside. All she did was scream until she decided to make an attempt for escape. By the time she went to make a break to escape, a sharp blade punctured the tent and came down on Angel, stabbing her in the collar bone area. She screamed in pain as the sharp blade continued to tear through the tent and stab Angel all over.

After the unknown party was finished with Angel, all that was left were 3 murdered corpses and a shredded bloody tent. The unknown party dragged Byron's lifeless body over to the tent and tossed him over what was once a tent, now a shredded, bloody cloth. They picked up their blunt object and bludgeoned Byron a few more times over the head.

When it was all over there was nothing, but a group of dead friends, beaten, stabbed and abused who lay in a shredded, bloody collapsed tent. A night of nothing, but fun came to an end with the reaper calling them home.

(After the Night- Following The Morning)

Coming down the trail was a young kid on a bicycle. Following behind him were two others on their bicycles as well. As they continued to ride down the trail, they came across two motorcycles that were parked off side of the trail. They stopped to admire the cycles.

"Wow! Cool bikes." The young child said, with enthusiasm.

"I want one so bad." The other young child spoke.

As they continued to admire the motorcycles, the one kid saw something from the distance. He was able to make out a man sleeping over his tent.

"Guys look!"

The children stared over at the man and started to laugh.

"Is he drunk?"

"Blayde, go and wake him up."

"No. You go and wake him up."

"I'm not going anywhere near him."

"Blayde and Cole, just leave the guy alone. Let's ride some more."

"Caiden always acts like he's the boss." Cole said as he rode away on his bike.

"He's your brother."

"I didn't ask for him."

"I can hear both of you."

"So what!" Blayde and Cole said, simultaneously.

The three children cruised away on their bicycles. They had no idea what they had just saw. The further down the trail they got, they almost hit another group of 3, bird watching on the trail. Caiden apologized to the bird watchers as Blayde and Cole continued to ride without acknowledging them.

The bird watchers would walk so far down the trail, stop and stare into their binoculars. The one man of the 3 was scouting with his set of binoculars and came across the sleeping, drunk man. As he watched him through the binoculars, he was able to tell that he was no sleeping, drunk man. He was a hurt man unconscious, or

dead, who lay over a bloody, tarnished
tent. The man became extremely alarmed and
frightened.

"Oh my God! Guys look!" The man
screamed as he ran towards the hurt man.

The other two men followed with him,
still not certain of what has made their
friend highly alarmed. Finally, reaching
the hurt man's presence, they realized that
they have just met horror. The three bird
watchers stood in shock. None of them
moved, and none of them talked. They could
not do anything.

They could tell that the man was not
alone. There were others, but the majority
of their bodies were covered by the
tarnished tent. The tent was cut up and
torn as if someone took a knife to it. The
man who lay over the tent was brutally
beaten and bludgeoned. His jaw appeared to
be broken, and his head was covered in
lacerations.

The bird watchers still standing in
shock, all they could see is the color red.
The beaten man lay in a pool of his own

blood, along with whomever lay dead with him. After the bird watchers came back into being, they were able to say that they discovered a group of people who were murdered. A group who were brutally beaten and stabbed to death in their tent. All of a sudden they became extremely frightened once more, when the beaten man suddenly moved.

"One of us has to go for help. I'll stay here, but somebody has to go for help." The discoverer said.

As 2 of the 3 bird watchers stayed back, the other ran for help to call 911. They were in awe. They had not a clue on what had just happened. Starring down at the red pile of bodies, the man slightly moaned from the little air that could escape from the blood in his mouth. As for the other bodies, they did not move. They could only see the feet of 2 bodies and the arm from another. The rest of their bodies were covered by the shredded, blood covered tent.

"What in the name of God happened here?" The discoverer asked.

"I don't know what to say..." The bird watcher said as he began to look around nervous, as if the person who done this gruesome attack was still lurking about. He continued to speak.

"I'm getting very scared being here right now. Whoever did this could be still around."

"We have to do this. We can't just leave. Jesus Christ, who deserves this?" He said, becoming emotional.

It was becoming hard for them to be a witness to such a heinous scene. This was an event that would traumatize them forever. Even looking away from the bodies, it would not leave their mind. Just a site of a brutally beaten dead bodies resting in a pool of their own blood. Not knowing why, or what happened picked at their brains like tics. Every minute to them seemed like an hour. They did not have the slightest clue of when their friend would return with the authorities. All they could do was wait and hope that it would be soon enough. One thing they witnessed and saw with their eyes was the absolute sign of a pure brutal, hateful and horrific happening.

(Present Time- 2004)

It was another quiet moment at the table. Byron sat with his head down, staring at the table. In some type of way he could not speak any more. Detective Wrighmas stared around the room and kind of fidgeted at the table.

"You honestly can tell me that the last thing you remember was Seth walking away to take a piss?" Asked Detective Wrighmas.

"I would tell you more if I did." said Byron answering the Detectives question.

"You don't remember being found? You don't even remember seeing anybody. Seth took a piss, that's it?"

"No, not really... The ambulance ride is a fade, but I can only tell you what I remember from the hospital. I tell you, it kills me not to know what came down that night. It literally eats me alive."

Detective Wrighmas became silent now. He began to think about what he could remember. It was his turn to speak about what he could remember. He started to think that if he did some explaining, more could come back to Byron remembering. It was beginning to become a tedious job for Detective Wrighmas, but he did not give up. He had the intuition that he was going to crack the Lake Bodom mystery. All he had to do was fill in the potholes of Byron's and make it to the end. Could he get Byron to remember a murder that he did commit, but blocked out the memory? Or could he get enough input from Byron's story to discover who the psychotic, cold blooded, murderer was?

Detective Wrighmas began his work of psychology by venting out his memory of that early morning in 1960.

"I can remember getting the call. I had to meet with the witness who put the call in. I wasn't even a full year on the force when that happened. I was the closest officer to the scene, the first officer to respond, and the first officer on site."

"That's quite impressive." Byron said, being sarcastic."

Detective Wrighmas ignored his sarcasm and just continued to talk.

"When the dispatcher called in we were informed that it was possibly two dead bodies and one alive, but critical. It was hard scene to look at. I was in awe when I saw what I saw. Believe me, still to this day after all the years I've been in law enforcement, that scene is still the most disturbing... I been to a number of murder scenes, and after forty years, it's still the worst I've seen, still the most disturbing, still the most hateful and still the most horrific murder scene I've been too."

Byron did not respond to anything Detective Wrighmas said about the murder scene. He kept silent and just listened to Detective Wrighmas's story. He listened as if he was going to sprout a new memory of what happened to them that night into early morning. Byron's brain did not produce a new memory, and Detective Wrighmas continued his story mode of what he could remember on that early morning in 1960.

(Past Time- 1960)

After an extremely long, lengthy foot travel, the birdwatcher managed to make it to a street pay phone. He was completely out of breath, and he was drenched in sweat. He was nearly dehydrated. He did not hesitate when he saw the pay phone. He immediately picked up the phone and made the emergency call. Only 1 ring and a dispatcher picked up. Being winded and sweating, he forced himself to say it all in 1 fast sentence.

"There has been a murder at the Lake Bodom! Possibly two maybe three!"

"What is your name sir?"

"Apostle Calvary."

"Are you at the scene?"

"No, but my two friends are. I ran to get help, and they stayed back."

"OK, and where is your location?"

"I'm in Kunnarla on Bodomintie."

"Did you say your friends are at the scene?"

"Yes, ma'am."

"I am going to send an officer to your location, and he will pick you up. I'm also going to send other officers to the scene, okay?

"Yes."

"OK, just hang in there for a while the police are on their way. We'll stay on the phone together, and you can let me know when the officer is in your presence."

"That's fine."

"Apostle, I know it's hard to talk about something else, but are you from the area?"

"I'm from Espoo."

"Oh, okay, so you're a little bit close."

"Yeah. We usually come every weekend and bird watch near the lake."

"That sounds like a fun."

Just only a few minutes later, Apostle was able to see a patrol unit pull up behind him next to the sidewalk. It stunned him to see an officer respond so quick and fast.

"Ma'am, the police officer is here now."

"Okay. Well good luck to you with everything and you are very brave. You hang in there I know this is very traumatic for you and you're going to pull through."

"Thank you ma'am. That means a lot to me."

"Now go with the police officer and cooperate the best you can. I know you'll do well."

"Thank you! Thanks a lot!"

Apostle hung up the phone, and the policeman was opening the passenger side door for him.

"Hey, what's up? I'm Officer Allen Wrighmas."

Apostle entered the vehicle and the officer closed the passenger door. Once Officer Wrighmas entered the vehicle, the patrol lights came on, and they were racing down the road to the heinous, murder scene at Lake Bodom.

"So, tell me kid... What did you see? What happened down there?"

"I saw a murder."

"You actually saw the murder?"

"No! I'm sorry. I didn't actually see the murder! We found them dead." Apostle answered, being as if he were offended or if the police officer was just stupid.

"How many are there?"

"What do you mean?" Apostle answered, growing confused.

"Dead! How many are dead?"

"I believe there are two, but there may be three. It's a bloody site. I'm talking a lot of blood. There are at least two dead inside of a tent, but there is one laying over the tent and I think he's still alive. There's just massive amounts of blood."

Apostle was beyond panic stricken. He was beyond scared. He was aflutter and dismayed.

"That bad, huh?"

"It's very bad... Horrific."

"Horrific? That's pretty damn serious." The officer said, being sarcastic.

Apostle could not understand why the policeman was being such an asshole. He just wanted to get this done and over with.

"I don't understand why you're being so sarcastic with me. People are dead. I'm sorry, but I don't deal with this kind of stuff on a daily basis."

Officer Allen Wrighmas ignored Apostle and just moved on with asking him questions.

"So, you said we... Who's we?"

"Myself and my two friends."

"What were the three of you doing down there... Jerking each other off, or something?"

"Yeah- Right... We were bird watching and we found them."

"Bird watching? Yeah just how many birds were you watching?" The officer laughed.

"Do you have some kind of problem with me for some reason, or are you just a born asshole? Some of the questions and comments you're making is unnecessary."

"I haven't quite figured that one out yet. Believe me, people ask me that almost every day."

"I think it would be best to just keep the rest of the ride quiet."

After a 6 minute ride which seemed like forever for Apostle, they finally made it on the location of the murder scene. Coming to the wooded area made Apostle grow even more afraid. Just knowing that he had to come back made his heart beat double in time. His adrenaline was flowing, and he had a lump in his throat the size of a boulder. He did not want to look at the gory scene any more.

It was a bit more dark on the location, being that the clouds moved in and covered the sun. It made their environment fit more for a horror film, and it camouflaged their reality, being that they were all in a state of denial. You could see that Apostle's two friends moved away from the scene and were standing more on the entering road, which ended by the trails and lake. There you could also tell that Wrighmas was the first officer on the scene. Officer Wrighmas parked his patrol unit and both parties exited. Officer Wrighmas began to approach the scene. Apostle reunited with his friends and just stood beside the 2 of them.

Once he made it into view, he immediately did not believe his eyes. He stood still and just stared at the site in recklessness. He began to specifically stare down at the boy who was grunting inertly and scarcely moving. Officer Wrighmas called in on his radio.

"Dispatch, I'm on location of the multiple 187, are there more officers on their way? I need an ambulance as soon as possible."

"Unit 13, there are officers in route, and that's affirmative with the ambulance."

Officer Wrighmas knelt down next to the brutally beaten and left for dead, young boy. He grabbed hold of his hand and held it.

"Hang in there bud. If you can, wiggle your fingers if you can hear me."

The half dead, young boy did not respond. Officer Wrighmas grew closer towards the shredded, tarnished bloody tent. He analyzed it for a moment, and he was able to realize that there were three bodies wrapped inside of what was left of what was once a tent.

After a short time period, the ambulance arrived as well as another patrol unit and an unmarked vehicle which was occupied by a detective. The detective came into being with Officer Wrighmas. The other officer stood back with the birdwatchers and was taking statements.

"Well, if it's not the rookie that gets to the crime scene first."

"What can I say? I love my job... Or was I just the closest officer?"

"Ha ha, you probably were the closest cop to the scene."

"That I was..."

"Tell me what we got."

"We got three dead in the tent, and one barely alive here."

The detective analyzed the live victim for a moment. He checked him out from head to toe, looking at all his wounds.

"We're going to have to look for a knife, or any object that could be used for stabbing. We definitely want to look for a branch, any type of stick... Any type of object that could be used for beating the fuck out of somebody with. We want to scout all over these woods for any rough play. There's no way in hell it all happened right here... Whoever it was who done this, was pretty pissed off... They enjoyed doing it too, I would like to add."

He stood up from the bloody victim, placing his hands on his hips. He starred around, looking at his surroundings.

"It's definitely a good idea to get him to a hospital. Hey, medics you can carry him out of here now!" He yelled at them, being rude while keeping his arrogant, self-important personality.

Once the beaten, young boy was removed from the blood painted murder scene, the detective's next move was for the tent. After some lifting and maneuvering, he was able to openly see the three abused corpses. The corpses were Seth, Angel and Amelia. For some, or no particular reason at all, someone took the lives of these young lovers and Byron, being the only 1 who barely survived.

Seth had stab wounds all over his body. He had repeated slashes in his back, he was stabbed in the face 3 times, and he was stabbed in the stomach 6 times and stabbed 7 times in the chest. He was beaten over the head several times with an unknown, blunt object. If the stab wounds to his chest did not kill him, it would have been the bludgeoning.

Angel was also savagely murdered. She had repeated stab wounds, in her chest, neck and head. Although she was gruesomely stabbed to death, Seth's death was more angry. It was possible that she was beaten with the blunt object and then killed by the stab wounds in her chest and head.

Amelia on the other hand, her death was an absolute raging expiry. The 1 held accountable for these 3 murders, took all the anger, frustration and irritability out on Amelia. She was bludgeoned just like the 3 others and beyond excessively stabbed. The lacerations from the stabbing led her to be mutilated. Her entrails were exposed, and it was likely that the murderer continued to stab her repeatedly, long after her death. The killing of Amelia was personal. All of the deaths could have been personal, but the look of Amelia's beaten, mutilated, abused corpse showed that she was their main focus.

There were even some pieces of her entrails all over the inside of the tent, on the ground and even on the other corpses. The scene of this crime was nothing, but an evil, horrific happening and leaving behind 3 brutally beaten bodies. Even though there was 1 remaining to survive the blood red, painted scene where a murder demon had lurked, there were 3 taken home by the reaper.

After such a happening, there was nothing left at the scene. The police and detectives recovered absolutely zip. They did not find a knife, or anything that could be used for a stabbing weapon. They could not even find the weapon used for the head bludgeoning. The 1 thing that twisted the brains of the police force was having no leads. They did not have 1 suspect, or any idea on who the person was who committed such an evil, horrific murder. With the 3 youngsters savagely murdered and 1 barely alive, there was nothing the police force could do for them, but to do whatever in their power to bring justice to this evil stranger. It was as if Satan, or 1 of his demons came up from hell and took them, leaving 1 behind. Or was it the Reaper, death itself coming to collect. However, Byron could be the 1 and only lead to opening and closing this whodunit.

(Present Time- 2004)

It was typically quiet once more at the table. Detective Wrighmas starred at Byron and Byron again, stared at the table with his head down. It was a long 2 minute silence until Detective Wrighmas chimed in.

"So what do you see Byron? Does that help you?"

"No, not really." He said, starting to cry.

"Can you imagine what I just told you? You still can't remember when you first encountered the killer?"

"No! Don't tell me that, I can't imagine it." Byron said, sadly crying.

"Do you feel lucky at all for pulling through and being able to survive?"

"No, I don't feel lucky at all. I feel unfortunate. She shouldn't have died that night. It should have been me."

"I think you were lucky. For some reason, that cold blooded killer didn't do on to you like he did them. You weren't nearly as hurt as your friends, but you were still pretty bad though. You were cut in the head pretty bad. You had a couple stabs on your body and was beaten in the head pretty good. You suffered a broken jaw with some heavy head trauma."

Byron just sat quiet, listening and shaking his head. No matter how hard he thought, he would draw a blank. It was screwing with his mind to not be able to draw up anything. He even closed his eyes and thought of the last thing he could remember, which Seth was having to get up to relieve himself. He kept drawing that memory in his head over and over again. He still could not bypass that particular moment of Seth walking away to urinate. He gave up trying anymore because no matter how hard he tried, he could not break past that point.

"I can't do it. I cannot remember anything from the point at the fire to the hospital. I draw a vague memory in the ambulance and have a blur at the hospital. What I do remember at the hospital, is you being there and you were explaining everything that happened to me. You waited to tell me about my friends. That is about the only thing I could honestly say that I remember clearly."

" Now how about that and look where we are now... Who ever thought that we would whined up like this? It's strange how the cards play out sometimes. I want to tell you something Byron. We're starting to run out of time. It's not going to be long now until either myself, or others are going to be transporting you to the jail."

"Well, if it's going to be anybody transporting me to jail, can I request that it's you taking me?"

"I'm sure I can make arrangements. But you have to listen to me Byron. You got to dig in your brain, and I mean deep. You have to try and give me some more. You need to find that inner wall and break past it. You can remember what happened."

"What more can you possibly want? I pulled together everything I could remember that night. I'm sorry I was beat in the head and can't remember a set point. It's how many years later? Now look what's happening to me. Now I'm the one being charged for murdering my friends and a woman who I loved! This is bullshit! It's bullshit, and I hope every last one of them in the justice system burn in damn hell! Burn in Goddamn hell!"

Byron was beginning to grow beyond upset. It was getting to the point to where he was going to stop cooperating, or just call it all quits with the detective. It was to a possibility that Byron could strike out in physical violence.

"Just settle down a bit there Byron. We all don't want to do something we both will regret." Detective Wrighmas said, being highly assertive back towards Byron.

Detective Wrighmas waited a few moments and allowed everything to calm down. Then he picked up again and started back with Byron.

"Think about how it looks Byron. You were beaten less savagely than the three of them. Not to mention the only one to survive. None other than your lover was

killed the most barbarous. They claimed
Amelia to be mutilated. Keep in mind she
was stabbed over a dozen times, and that
was after the fatal blow..."

"You said it yourself that you believe
in my innocents."

"You're right I did say that, but that
doesn't help you in court at all. I'm
telling you the facts against you. Draw
something up! Give me something to help
you... With the facts against you, you can
be found guilty. Now if it was Angel or
Seth, you may have a leg to stand on, but
it's not. Amelia your lover, was found
stabbed, bludgeoned and mutilated. Her
lover Byron, you, still alive. You're
suspect. It's amazing they didn't bring you
in forty four years ago... All I'm saying
Byron is to look at the facts against you.
Not the evidence... The facts are what's
important in this matter."

"Screw the facts! There is no evidence
against me, and you cannot convict me on
facts. I believe whatever happens in the
end, will be what the turn out should be...

I said it once, and I'll say it again, what's done is done... It's just a shame that you couldn't have got the lemonade man."

"He checked out clean and so did the other guy. We investigated it. There is not one single suspect out there. You are the only suspect."

"Yeah, forty four years later... I'm appalled, and this is ludicrous. This is nonsense bullshit. You're right. What took them so long? What a good way to screw with somebody's life."

"I'm sorry Byron, but this is what the system came up with, and this is what my job is. In reality, my job is to scare the hell out of you and get you to confess. What I decided to do with you was different. I chose to give you the opportunity to tell your story. I thought to myself if there was anybody out there who could put this everlasting, murder mystery to a rest, it had to be you. I gave you the chance to get your mind prepped to get to the bottom of this uncommon murder.

Now we're to a point of no return. There isn't going to be much I can do for you any longer. We're going to have to wrap this up very soon. If there isn't much further for you to go, but a blank memory, we're going to have to move forward."

"Move forward... As in like what?"

"Like I have a wife to get home to and a very good dinner. My day is just about wrapped up."

"So that's it, you're going home?"

"Yes I am."

"Now what am I supposed to do?"

"I'll leave it up for you to decide. I can still hold you here for questioning, or I can go ahead and transfer you to jail. What would you like to do?"

"I'm really not sure. We're at a stalemate. I told you everything I can possibly remember."

"I think you can cough up some more. I'm going to let you sleep it off here. I'll let them know to get some grub in here for you. Sleep it off in the cell tonight and when I come back tomorrow, we'll get a fresh start... Stop holding back. I can look in your eyes and know there's more."

Byron kept quiet. Detective Wrighmas stood up from the table and walked towards the door.

"I'll make sure you get some grub."

Detective Wrighmas exited the room and called it a day at work. He was really determined to break through and finally solve the Lake Bodom murders. In his mind, he knew that Byron was withholding details from that night in 1960. He was going to come back to work the next day and hope to have a clean start with Byron and he would be able to continue where he left off from his story.

Later that night at the station Byron was escorted to a cell, where he would be detained for the remainder of the night. Once he was secured in his cell, Byron just sat quietly. He picked at his brain and was reliving the night at Lake Bodom all over again. It was to the point to where he

could not stop thinking about it. It was
him, alone in his cell, with just his
thoughts. Not to mention the smell of old
skunked booze and body odor from other
arrests. He grew tired and still did not
stop thinking about it hours later. It
played on his mind to when he fell asleep,
it grew to a dream. He grew adjusted to his
environment and was exhausted enough to
fall dead to the world. Not anything in the
world could wake him up. Not even a bomb.

(Past Time- 1960 Dreaming the story)

It was pretty silent once the ladies
retired to the tent for the night. With a
bright fire going and plenty of booze,
Byron and Seth were still being occupied,
with their beer and themselves. They were
nonstop carrying conversation after
conversation, beer after beer and many
laughs. It was a shame for all the fun they
were having and how soon it would all come
to an end. Without knowing what was soon
ahead of them, they would come to find

themselves in a doomed and fated state of
affairs.

The woods had eyes, and they were
drawn on to the camping site. Slickly
watching every move from drunken Byron and
drunken Seth. The eyes would eventually,
but slowly set in at a much more closer
distance. Byron and Seth had not the
slightest clue that they were being watched
and followed. They were being stalked as if
they were a lion's prey.

With Byron and Seth not knowing, they
just carried out with what they've been
doing the last few hours, which was
drinking and being drunk.

"You don't plan on passing out anytime
soon do you?" Seth asked Byron, with a slur
in his words.

"Not any time soon. Why?"

"Do you want to hit the trails and
burn one up?"

"It don't sound like a bad idea. Let's
just throw some more wood on this fire, so
it don't burn low while were gone."

After tending to the fire both of them headed for the trails. After they got so far down Seth ignited their essential object. After he took the first drag, they continued to further down the trail and then Byron started up another conversation.

"I have to say man we have to make a routine of this. I'm wanting to stay another night." He said.

"Yeah we can do it. We can make it like an every weekend type thing."

"Yeah we should make it an every weekend thing. One night isn't enough."

"Yeah. I think the ladies would like it to."

They stopped by a large rock. Big enough to make a seat on it. They both sat down, still burning their party favor.

"Speaking of the ladies' man, I have to have a heart to heart conversation with you." Byron said.

Seth grew immediately interested.

"Well, hit me with it man. This sounds pretty deep." He said with enthusiasm

"I catch you eyeballing Lia, a lot. I know you like her. I think she knows it too. I wanted to wait to talk to you about it, but now seems like a good time."

"Wow man. This is some heavy stuff."

"I'm being serious. I really like her, we made love for the first time tonight. She's really into me too. I know it's been only a few weeks, but we're really burning for each other, and I'd appreciate it if you would stop."

"Hey man, I'm sorry if I'm making you feel that way, but I don't mean any harm by it. It's a nature's habit, and we all do it, but I'm not in love or like your lady. I told you she was cute, and that's it."

"I know, but there's a difference between the natures habit and lusting another girl. I don't do it to you so don't do it to me."

Seth really guarded down from Byron's confront.

"I'm really sorry man. I'm glad you came to me about this. Like I said though, I definitely don't mean any harm by it. I guess I should try and control myself more... At least around your girlfriend."

"That's what I'm talking about man. I'm being serious."

Seth burst out laughing.

"I know man... I know. I'm just screwing with you."

From out of nowhere, in the distance a high pitch scream echoed in the woods. Both parties not really paying attention didn't give too much thought about it.

"That was a pretty freaky sound." Seth said, getting nervous from the noise.

"Yeah I wonder where that came from."

"What the hell was it?"

"Sounds like we may have some ghosts."

The sound spread through the woods once more and grew louder.

"That's starting to freak me the hell out man." Byron said.

"Do you want to start heading back?"

"Yeah I definitely think we should."

They both got up from the rock and carried a fast paced walk back to their campsite. As they gained a further distance the high pitch scream became more distinguishing. They both turned to each other.

"Dude, that's the girls' man!" Screamed Seth.

"Really?" Byron said, in denial.

"It sounded more like Angel."

Still hearing the screams as they grew louder, they both sprinted as fast as they could down the dark trail. Seth fell hard on his face being that it was too hard to see anything. Byron pulled Seth up from the ground.

"Come on man get up! Someone's hurting them!" Byron screamed in fear.

"Don't worry about me! Keep running." Seth yelled at Byron, in the middle of pulling him up.

Then before you knew it, the screaming stopped. You no longer heard the screams. They just immediately stopped.

"I don't hear them anymore. They stopped." Seth said.

"They were screaming pretty hysterical man. Like they were being hurt or something."

"Maybe it was an animal, and it scared the shit out of them."

They both stopped running. They were now much closer to their campsite. They could see the light and glare from their camp fire.

"Well, I'm sure if someone was killing them they'd still be screaming right?" Seth said laughing.

"Yeah, were pretty close now. It probably was just some animals. They're probably wondering where we went to."

"We should sneak up on them. That would be priceless."

"No, we can't do that. They just got the shit scared out of them. Now we'll scare the shit out of them? We can't do that."

"I know, but it would be hilarious."

They were now approaching the fire but did not see the ladies. There was no sign of them. As they approached their site even closer, They then discovered that their tent was collapsed.

"Okay what now man? What the hell is going on?" Asked Seth.

"Lia!"

There was no response and still no sign of Amelia and Angel.

"Girls!" Yelled Seth at the top of his lungs.

As they approached the tent, they saw that it had been shredded, and it was covered in blood. They were thunderstruck.

"Jesus Christ man! Oh my God what happened!" Seth cried as he fell to his knees.

From nowhere all that could be seen, was a hand holding an extremely, sharp blade reach out and stab Byron right in the stomach. He instantly fell backwards as the blade struck him in the chest. Then once more in his head. Once he hit the ground, a long blunt object came down and struck him in his face. Then once more, but only this time it broke his jaw. It did not stop from there. The unknown party continued to strike him with the blunt object.

The unknown attacker also had his way with Seth. By the time Seth recovered from being emotional and saw Byron being attacked, the unknown party bashed him, widespread across his face with a long blunt object. Byron still lay on the ground limp and did not move one single nerve in his body. He was bleeding out, and the only

person who could save him was in the same
position. Seth was immediately unconscious
from the unexpected blow and lay sprawled
out on the ground. The long object come
down on his face one more time. That was
the strike that broke every bone. It was
not over for Seth either at this point.
After countless blows with the blunt
object, is when the hand of doom came down
with the pointed object. As Seth lay
completely defenseless on the ground, he
began to be stabbed over and over again.
One after the other. Then before you knew
it, Seth had given up the ghost. Byron's
lifeless body, which lay only 20 feet from
Seth's corpse and the shredded tent, where
the ladies corpses were slain.

Both of their bodies were even dragged
over to the tent, and that is where their
corpses would be stuffed along with the
young and beautiful ladies who were left
dead, beaten and stabbed to death. This was
not just a murder. This was not just a
horrifying action, but a massacre to 4
lovers who shared a night of fun. There
cannot be any given explanation to justify

what happened to the young and bright
lovers who would have a fresh start for
their future.

(Moments ago)

The ladies were sound to sleep in
their tent. With Byron and Seth being away
from the campsite, the sound toned down.
The only noise you could hear besides the
night creatures was the wood burning in the
fire. With the ladies being asleep in the
tent, all alone, with their companions a
distance away, the reaper was coming to
collect.

All of a sudden the tent was being
thrashed at and cut open. A hand with the
pointed object made its way through and
began to savagely stab Angel while she was
sleeping. Barely able to wake up, she died
shortly after the repeated blows to her
chest, a countless amount of times. Her
blood began to paint the inside of their

tent. The blood spread enough to where Amelia was covered with it.

Amelia was finally woken up to Angel being attacked. She immediately started frantically screaming. That is when she tried to escape from the tent, but she was tucked in the corner. With Angel still being attacked, Amelia managed to find a way out of the tent. Still screaming as she fought her way through the shredded tent, she took off running as fast as she could, not even knowing which direction she was going..

Amelia was running as fast as she could and screaming as loud as she could. Her screams were so loud it echoed through the entire woods and lake area. Amelia was on the run for her life. She did not have the slightest clue what she had just witnessed. She continued to run and had no idea where she was heading. She just ran because she knew he had to get away to save her life.

Amelia ended up getting a feel for relief that she was getting away. She felt

that she ran so fast and made it so far to
where she would get away. For that brief
moment of relief, it was taken away when
suddenly out of nowhere, she was gripped by
her hair and stabbed repeatedly in her
back. She fell to the ground not able to
make a sound, or scream anymore. She was
then dragged back to the tent area by her
hair, where Angel's body lay brutally
stabbed to death. Amelia was still alive
but was hanging on by a thread. The stab
wounds in her back were severe and her
lungs were also punctured from the stab
wounds being so intense. She could not get
a weep out. She was slowly bleeding out and
suffocating.

After being dragged back to the tent
site, she was then tossed back inside what
was left of the tent along with Angel's
abused corpse. Once she was placed inside
of the tent, along sharpened object came
down hard, slicing her open. Not just 1
time, or 2 times, or even 3 times, but a
countless number of times. This was a
tempered anger, along with a passion to

continue to slice and stab another human
being and enjoy doing it.

Before you knew it Amelia was dead and
lay right next to her dear friend. Both
savagely beaten left for dead and alone in
their broken tent. It was only a matter of
time until Byron and Seth would soon join
their lovers. For Byron and Seth, they had
not the thinnest hint what they were
heading for when they would arrive back at
their campsite. The reaper would be there
to greet Byron and Seth. They only had
minutes counting down on their lives. By
the time they reached their campground,
Amelia and Angel were already brutally
attacked and killed. Not long after they
discovered their lover's bodies, they soon
became victims themselves. When the night
was over the four companions became
lifeless victims by the early morning.

However, there was just 1 person who
happen to survive the evil and horrifying
brutal murders, and it was Byron Niles.
After Byron Niles was found, he suffered
from multiple stab wounds and severe head
trauma. He also suffered from a broken jaw.

Why was Byron Niles so fortunate to survive an unbearable event? For some reason or another, the reaper did not take him home with his friends or lover. Does the Reaper make mistakes? Or was it just not his time to pass through the life stage?

What really happened and who really was it that committed these gruesome attacks? Was it really and truly the reaper, or just some crazed mad man who went on a psycho holiday? The answer has yet to be answered.

Whoever it was left horror and stained the Lake Bodom with blood forever. Who was it? Will anyone ever know? Many years have passed... Too many years were silent. Whoever it is, is soon bound to reappear. It's inevitable, they have to onslaught again. They could not be done. Sooner or later something kindred would happen again.

(Present Time- 2004)

The sun had risen, and it was a new day. Detective Wrighmas stood, watching Byron inside the cell sleeping. He held a coffee in each hand along with a small white bag.

"Byron, good morning!" He yelled.

Byron startled awake. He looked around and stared up at Detective Wrighmas. He was still half asleep.

"What time is it?" Byron asked.

"It's seven 0clock... A.M. It's time to get up. We have some wrapping up to do today."

Detective Wrighmas let Byron out of the cell and escorted him back to the interrogation room. They both sat back at the table. Detective Wrighmas opened up the white bag and pulled out a breakfast bagel sandwich wrapped in foil. He slid the sandwich and coffee to Byron.

"Here, I got you a coffee along with an egg and sausage bagel."

"Thanks a lot. I'll definitely eat it. I love coffee by the way."

"So, let's get down to brass tax. Did you think anything over?"

Byron dug into the bagel.

"I thought a lot over."

"Is that so?"

"I didn't figure a whole lot out, but I was able to come up with some more."

"See Byron? I told you you'd be able to come up with more. Tell me what you have for me."

"We left our campsite. Myself and Seth. We took a walk down the trail and hung out at this rock for a little while."

"And the girls?"

"They stayed asleep in the tent. I remember hearing the screams."

"The screams? Who was screaming?"

"It was the girls... At least to me it sounded like Amelia. When we first heard them, we couldn't distinguish what it exactly was. For a second, it scared us. Then we were able to tell it was the girls. We ran back, and when we got there the tent was shredded and collapsed."

"OK, were making it. Keep it rolling."

"I'm running out. I think I recall getting stabbed here," and he pointed to his stomach. "That is when I could have been hit in the head."

"What about Seth?"

"I don't remember. I see a hand and a long object. It could be a branch. Maybe a pipe. I'm not certain."

Detective Wrighmas sat quiet for a brief moment. He replayed in his head what he had just heard.

"Understand something Byron. Everything you're saying, they're going to use against you. So you need to make sure that you have everything clear and ready to explain to a judge and jury. You can't play the "I don't remember card."

"I'm not playing the "I don't remember card". I'm telling you everything I remember. There isn't much to tell anymore."

"Are you really saying that?"

"Yes, I'm really saying that. I didn't see the ladies get murdered. I didn't see Seth get murdered. I see a hand and a long object. Such as a branch, or a pipe. I recall somewhat being stabbed. It's plain and simple. There was somebody else there that night. We saw a man alone, somebody threw rocks at us, and somebody killed us."

Byron was growing upset.

"Calm down Byron."

"How? How am I supposed to be calm? I've been calm long enough. There is nothing more to tell."

"Do you want a moment to calm down, and we'll get back at it?"

"There's nothing to get back at. You said we had some wrapping up to do. Well, I think we about wrapped everything up."

"Okay, Byron. You said it yourself. I'm going to need you to stand up now and place your hands behind your back."

Byron stood up and followed his directions.

"Shouldn't you need a uniform for this?"

"No, but I can get the uniformed officers to do this for me, and I can go home on an early day. I was transporting you on a favor you asked."

Detective Wrighmas placed the handcuffs on to Byron and escorted him out of the room, taking him to a patrol unit. Once they were outside, Byron caught a familiar feeling.

"You know this weather can remind me of that night."

"It does, does it?"

"It's comfortable little gusts of wind. Nice and warm. Not too hot."

"You can remember that pretty well. Too bad you couldn't remember anything else that well."

Detective Wrighmas assisted Byron into the unit. Making sure he didn't hit his head, he closed the door and entered on his side. He watched Byron through the rear view mirror. He was able to tell Byron was feeling down. He started the vehicle and drove off.

"You know Byron, I hope this goes well for you."

"I don't care what happens. I just wanted to be left alone. I never fully moved on from that night, but to suddenly reopen it all again... It's hard to deal with mentally."

"I can only imagine."

"I don't think you can imagine."

"You know, you're probably right. I probably can't walk in your shoes."

"No you can't. I just wanted to be left alone."

"Maybe once this is over you can be left alone and have your peace."

"You may be half right, but I'll have my peace when I'm dead."

"Why do you say that?"

"I haven't had peace in over forty years."

"Are you trying to say that you've haven't put this behind you? You've been carrying this with you this long?"

"I guess you can say that. You can be right on that mark."

"You have to learn to let that go. That's not a good way to live your life. It's bad for your health." "It's easier said than done. You have no idea."

"Right. Let's not go down that road again."

"Right. Let's not."

"However Byron, there is one road I would like to go down. On your behalf, I held back from asking you." "Now, tell me. What is it that you would like to ask me?"

"What did you think when you found out how Amelia was killed?"

"What exactly do you mean?"

"She was brutalized and mutilated. She was stabbed a bunch of times even after she was dead." "Is this the big thing you wanted to ask me?"

"Yes it is. You survived with less severe wounds, and your lover died a brutal death. What do you think about that?" "There's not much to think about. I don't know what to tell you."

"That's not much of an answer."

"It's not a subject that I really have to discuss with you. This is all an opinionated conversation." "That's fine Byron. You don't have to share any of it with me. You can just relax the rest of the way there." "I think that's what I'll do."

(An Alternate Aspect- 1960)

Byron and Seth sat on a rock, sharing their essential cigarette. They talked about a lot of things, but one subject in particular which Byron brought forward. "Seth, listen to me man. I see you eyeing up Amelia. On top of the things you said to me, I'd appreciate it if you kept it all to yourself." "Wow, man. There's something I want to mention to you too. Amelia and myself have liked each other for a while now. This is even before you two hooked up." "How long has this been going on?"

"Nothing is really going on. We just like each other."

"Does Angel know anything about this?"

"She knows I like her. She doesn't know Amelia likes me because that would cause shit between them." "This is some dirty bullshit Seth."

"Relax man."

"Relax? I'm in love with a girl, and there's all this bullshit going on behind my back! You're supposed to be my friend!

What the fuck!" "I'm sorry man. Feelings
are feelings, and they're hard to control.
You're my friend, and I care about you."
Byron stared around as if he was looking
for a weapon. He spotted a rock on the
ground. A rock big enough to use as a
weapon, while holding it. He discretely
picked it up from the ground. Seth was
still sitting on the rock. Byron stood with
his back turned. "You're right Seth.
Feelings are hard to control."

"Are you Okay man?"

Byron turned and bashed the rock,
directly across Seth's skull. Seth already
sitting, fell face down into the dirt and
did not move. Byron just stood still,
staring down at Seth's lameness body. Seth
was severely bleeding from his skull. He
lay as if he was dead. From the distance,
Byron heard screaming. It was the voice of
a female, and she was calling out. After a
few more times of hearing the woman's
voice, he was able to make out that it was
Angel. He immediately stared back down at
Seth. Seeing that he was not moving, he
abandoned his friend and ran towards the

campsite. Byron was sprinting down the
trail. Still hearing Angel call out for
them, he began to call back. "Angel!
Angel!"

"Seth!"

He made it into her view. He was
sweating and breathing real hard. He
grabbed hold of Angel. "Are you Okay? Did
you find Seth?"

"No! I thought he was with you."

"He wasn't. Where's Amelia?"

"She's still sleeping. I just woke up.
I was wondering where you guys went."

"You are all liars, Angel." Byron
said, growing furious.

"What are you talking about?"

"You lied to me, and now you're going
to answer for it."

"Byron what's gotten into you?"

Byron slapped Angel across her face,
sending her to the ground.

"Oh my God! What are you doing!" She yelled, as she attempted to stand back up. Byron then booted her stomach and caused her to fall back down. The wind was knocked out of her. You could hear Angel attempt to take a breath, but she could not get any air into her lungs from how hard he kicked her.

Byron broke off a sizable branch from a tree. He was waiving it back and forth in front of Angel's face. Angel was finally able to catch her breath. She burst out" crying.

"Byron, stop! Byron, stop! Amelia help! Help!" She screamed in distress.

"Nobody is going to help you. Your lover boy, you know the one who wants to fuck my lady? He's lying dead so far down the trail, and now it's going to be you." "What? Seth's dead!" She cried.

Byron raised up the branch and came down hard, striking Angel's abdomen, knocking her wind out once more. All she could do was lay there and attempt to fight for the air to come back into her lungs.

She tried to crawl away, but he then raised the branch again and came down harder, but this time bashing her in the face. After the contact, Angel lay sprawled out and unconscious. After all her ribs, nose and jaw getting broken, there was no more cries, or movement coming from Angel. Her skull was bashed in, and she was bleeding out. Byron tossed down the branch and pulled out a sharp blade. He then stood over her and began to stab Angel numerous times. When he was done he took a small breather. He glanced over at the tent and began to storm towards it, knowing Amelia was inside. He was an infuriated man with murder on his mind. Behind his hateful mood and furious anger, was a hurt man. His heart was broken by the woman he loved and his best friend. Rather being a man of understanding and to just move past the situation, he became a reaper of evil. Nothing was to stop him. Byron tripped on a book bag, walking to the tent. He looked down and saw that it was Seth's hiking bag. It then refreshed his memory that Seth packed a blade with him. He set down the blade he just killed Angel with. After dumping out the bag, he picked up not just an ordinary blade. This blade was a bayonet. Once it was in his possession, he didn't even enter the tent. He just thrashed at it. After shredding the tent open, he came down with the blade and stabbed Amelia in the chest. For a brief second, her eyes opened as blood spurted from her mouth. After that brief moment, Amelia was dead. Byron did not stop there. He continued to stab Amelia over and over again in the chest, moving to her stomach. He then continued to stab Amelia in the stomach, exposing her entrails. He continued to stab her enough to where he began to drench sweat and tire his arm.

By this time Amelia was nothing, but a battered bloody corpse painted with her own blood. Byron was a bloody madman with a blade hovering over an abused corpse. All of a sudden, Byron heard movement. He quickly turned his head to see that Angel was beginning to move. He stood up and began to walk towards her. When he went to take his first step, he looked down at Amelia and stomped down on her neck,

breaking it as he walked over to finish
Angel off. He walked over and stomped down
on her stomach. Angel coughed up blood from
her mouth. She put all effort into moving,
but still barely moved. Byron took the
blade and stuck it to her throat. Just as
he was going to slit her throat, he got
bashed in the back of his skull with a long
object. It caused him to fall to the
ground, dropping his blade.

"You sick bastard!" The voice cried
out.

It turned out that Seth was not dead
after all. He was just knocked unconscious.

"Byron, what the fuck did you do man?"
Seth said in anger, denial, and sadness as
he cried. Byron slowly stood up from the
ground and staggered a bunch. He lamely
walked towards Seth. "You are all getting
what you deserve!" He yelled.

Seth stood still, holding the branch
and watching Byron. Seth was completely
horrified and did not believe what was
happening before his eyes. Once he was able
to take in and accept what was happening

around him, Seth was ready to do what he had to do. He bashed Byron once more with the branch. It came across his face, breaking his jaw. Byron fell back to the ground, and Seth bashed him once more on the head. Seth dropped the branch and picked up the blade. He raised up the blade and was ready to stick Byron with it, but suddenly stopped. He lowered his hand. He starred down at Byron and saw that he was the one now laying on his back, out cold and defenseless. He dropped the blade and then dropped to his knees as he reached out to hold Angel. Seth burst into tears, holding Angel's broken body.

"Oh, Angel. Baby, I'm here. Baby, I'm here. I'm going to get you out of here. I'm with you now. I'm so sorry I couldn't help you." Seth continued to cry hysterical like a neglected and deprived baby. Seth attempted to lift her up and carry her, but he was much too afraid to move her. Angel was hurt badly. All of her ribs were broken, her nose and jaw was broken. Her mouth was filling with blood, and there was a good chance she could have brain trauma.

"I'm going to get help. I'm going to ride out on my bike, and I'm going to bring help. Don't worry, I'll be back for you." Seth said, continuing to cry. Without his knowledge, Byron made it to his feet and stabbed Seth in the back. Seth screamed and fell, rolling on to his back. Byron came down, stabbing Seth in his stomach. Seth grabbed the wrist of Byron and was beginning to fight back. Byron continued to stab down at Seth while Seth fought to prevent the blade from entering him. Seth discovered a sharp object and grabbed possession of it. It was the original blade he used to stab Angel. Seth stabbed at Byron, striking his chest area. Byron fell to his knees, and Seth stabbed at him once more with possession of the blade. He began to stab Byron, repeatedly. Byron fell to his back, but managed to get possession of the branch once more. Seth stood up, holding the blade out to Byron. "You crazy psychotic son of a bitch! I'm going to kill you twice!."

That very second after Seth gave his bold statement, Byron swung the branch and was able to strike Seth in the face. Seth fell to the ground unconscious once again. Byron stood up and then finished Seth off. Byron stood over him and repeatedly began to beat Seth over the head with the branch. Not once, not twice, not three times, but a series of bashes to Seth's head. After the long heroic fight that Seth gave, it was unfortunate that in the end, it was Byron standing on his feet with two stabbed and bludgeoned corpses. He then looked down at Angel and realized that she was still alive, and he had to finish her. He threw down his blood stained branch and picked up his blade. He walked over to her and then knelt down on top of her. That is when he began to stab her. He stabbed her four times in the stomach and then stopped. He turned back to his branch. Angel, still barely breathing, that is when he finished her with the branch. He came down bashing her in the head with the branch six more times. At that point, Angel then gave up the ghost after taking such an intense beating. He took his time doing it, but he dragged Seth and Angel's corpses back to the shredded, bloody tent where Amelia's

mutilated corpse lay. He cleaned up just
about as much as he could and then he lay
down over the three corpses that were once
his friends, and went to sleep. What was
Byron going to do next? Did he have a plan?
Was he even going to try and attempt a
getaway, or did he not care if he was to
get caught for the murders he just
committed against his friends and his
significant other? They were found just
hours later by birdwatchers. Byron was
counted as the only survivor out of a group
of four. Byron was not considered a suspect
what so ever. Seth and Angel were
pronounced dead by being stabbed, beaten
and bludgeoned. Amelia was pronounced dead
by stab wounds and mutilation. Byron was
found with stab wounds, head trauma, and a
broken jaw. He is a survivor and considered
lucky.

(Present Time- 2004)

    Detective Wrighmas snapped out of a
day dream. His mind really began to shoot
with thoughts. Byron was sitting with his

legs rested across the seat. He was as comfortable as he could be in the back seat of a patrol car. "For the first time detective, you're awfully quiet." Byron stated.

"I'm just resting my brain that's all."

"Resting your brain? I didn't know detectives did that sort of thing."

"They really don't. You know Byron, I am really trying to play out what happened there. I really want to believe your innocence, I do." "Then all you have to do is believe me. It's after all these years, and they turn to me. I'm sure one of their past suspects was them, but whoever it was slipped through your fingers." "They all had solid, concrete alibis. They all checked out clean. Even the few who said they did it." "How did you let Kiosk Man slip away? If he was the stone thrower and hated the campers, how did you not nail him?" Byron yelled, becoming frustrated. "It's more complicated than you think, Byron."

"He hated the campers, he threw rocks... and he killed my friends. It was him. If not then it was one of the suspects." "Listen Byron. Kiosk Man is Val Karstrom. He was a prime suspect. There was not much being that he drowned himself in the lake in 1969." "I didn't know that."

"Yep. Val did himself in the lake. We talked with his neighbor who even said that he heard him say it himself, "I killed them." They were drinking when he said it. They had a well and his relatives stated that Val had filled in the well, and that's where the murder weapons were buried." "I take it you didn't find it."

"There was no murder weapon in the well, or anywhere on the property. Even after speaking with his wife, she stated that there was no way he could have done it." "How so?"

"The night it happened, he never left home. She was supposedly up through the night and he was in the bed sleeping next to her. There was no solid evidence we could pin against him, besides the hearsay.

We looked at it as drunk talk and bullshit." "But what about the guy in the hospital? How did he manage to slip?"

"The guy in the hospital... That was Andy Hansman. That was a strange suspect. He came in wearing clothes stained with blood. There was not much to link to that one." "Oh, but there is plenty on this one. Tell me detective, why do you hold out on this guy?" "There's nothing to hold out on By!"

Byron laughed a bunch.

"Then I guess I know more than you, or you're really a low down, shallow, lying bastard." "Damn Byron. Do you have any more?"

"Oh, hell yeah! I can go on and on. A lying son of a bitch, a coward, corrupt, lying pig!" "I'm starting to feel your anger. Just try and relax now."

"Just try and relax? You're the one who's lying to me." Byron said, becoming very furious and frustrated. "How am I lying to you, Byron? I told you there wasn't much we were able to do with him. He was drunk and on drugs. His clothes were stained up with blood..." Byron cut him off in mid-sentence,

"Did you forget to mention that the blood on his clothes wasn't his blood?"

Detective Wrighmas did not answer his question. He remained silent as Byron continued to stress his perspectives. "The guy was a spy for Christ's sake. Why didn't you guys take the clothes?

Detective Wrighmas was still speechless. There was not much for him to say. He could not defend himself only because Byron knew the truth. "You're being pretty quiet up there D.W. There is one thing I can't forget to mention... None of you ever questioned anybody. You barely got anything from the doctors and the only guy you questioned and released, was a man linked to five other murders. Where is he D.W." "We couldn't hold him. We had to let him go because there was nothing to hold him for. On top of it all, he came to the hospital prior to the murder time." "How can you figure? You have no idea what time that happened. You don't release a guy with bloodstained clothes and linked to five other murders... Including Kylee Sorrina." "I can't really talk about that one. I wasn't on the force yet. There was nothing we could to with him." "It's because he was juiced in. It's because of the spy job."

"Understand Byron, he was in that hospital hours before your event."

"You keep saying that but really, how do you really know?"

"Your friends were killed around the four, four thirty A.M. time. Andy Hansman entered the hospital at twelve fifteen A.M." "It's still too damn strange, and a coincidence."

"I'm sorry Byron. I really am sorry."

"Like you really give two shits what happens to me?"

"I would hate to see somebody with a good sense of innocence go down for it, and I would hate to see that person take a ride on the lightening." "To me it doesn't matter anymore. Whatever happens, happens. Although, I do believe that whatever does happen, will be the rightful turn out in the end." Detective Wrighmas began to think to himself for a moment. There was a few things running through his mind. One of them was considering a delay in the transporting. He wanted to stop and make a curious phone call, but he did not act on it. What he did act in on was the information regarding another suspect. "You know Byron, there was another suspect, but it was too tenuous to stand."

"What are you talking about?"

"Do you remember Peter Soiney?"

"A little bit."

"What do you know?"

Byron giggled and shook his head.

"That guy was always in trouble. He was caught for every type of crime there is. I know he was arrested for assault and robbery a few times. He was busted for burglarizing a lot of homes to." "Do you know any more?"

"I think that about sums, him all up right there."

"Well, allow me to fill in the rest... Peter hung himself at a prisoner transport station thirty five, plus years ago. He lived very close to the lake." "He did?"

"Yes he did. Here's the mind blower. He confessed to the Lake Bodom murders."

"Are you serious? What the hell!"

"This guy wasn't important, and he couldn't stand the charge."

"What are you talking about? This doesn't make any sense! This guy could have been it, and he's let off? He couldn't stand the charge. Your ass is itchy." "Listen Byron! The guy wasn't right. We interrogated him. His confession was weak, and he was drunk. There wasn't much weight to what he stated. He was very esoteric and wasn't much stable in the brain. We couldn't take his confession. He was considered incoherent, and it couldn't stand." "Then that is just some jive bullshit."

"I'm sorry Byron."

"That was better off not being said."

"Why is that?"

"That was just adding salt to the wound."

Detective Wrighmas started laughing.

"I'm glad someone can have a good time."

"I'm sorry Byron. I will tell you this, I am going to speak with an old friend of mine..." "Okay... and what does that do for me?"

"It may help you for court... This man is a dear friend of mine and he worked your case over 40 years ago." "What's this going to do for me?"

"I'm going to look over all of the old case files. I'm going to get a hold of my old pal Darius and see if there's any way we can build a little bit of hope for you. Maybe we can figure out if this could have been done by more than one person."

"Well, I do appreciate your help and you going out of your way."

"It's not all for you. I am also doing this so we can all finally get to the bottom. It would be nice to crack this case. What a solid favor is for you, is putting in the words that you're not a threat to anybody, or a high risk. You'll still be in here, but after forty days of evaluation they can let you out on supervision. Just don't do anything stupid, like flee and move to another country." "I highly doubt I would do anything like that. There's nothing to flee from. Like I said, my innocence will show in the end." So far in the distance the signs directing to the prison were coming closer. It was two miles until they would reach their destination. "Were pretty close now." Detective Wrighmas said.

"Oh, I'm just so thrilled."

"Just try and relax Byron. I know where you're going isn't any picnic. Just try and suck it up until they can release you." "Everything is easier said than done, but I will be fine."

Before Byron knew it, they were driving through the gate and entering the prison ground. Byron was a bit nervous, but he hid his feelings pretty well. Detective Wrighmas put the vehicle to a stop, and two guards approached the vehicle. They took Byron out of the vehicle, cuffed and shackled him. "Are all these chains really necessary?" Byron asked.

The guards ignored him.

"It's all part of the procedure Byron." Detective Wrighmas said.

The guards walked Byron to the entrance door for transported prisoners. Detective Wrighmas followed. Once they were inside, Byron and Detective Wrighmas parted ways. He watched Byron being escorted down a long hallway. The guards took him to a close by cell, and that was the last Detective Wrighmas saw from Byron Detective Wrighmas turned in the paperwork to the lady at the desk. He answered a series of questions and stated Byron's stability. He used a nearby phone and made a phone call to a friend. "Hello."

"Hey Darius. It's Allen."

"Allen, how are you doing?"

"I'm doing well. Can't complain. I'm actually calling you to see if we can talk about one of the old cases." "One of the old cases? Why do you want to do that of all things?"

"Well, it is one in particular, and I thought you may be able to help me a little bit."

"What one in particular, Allen?"

"It is the blood murders at Lake Bodom."

"Oh! An interesting one."

"You see, I'm at the jail. I just transported Byron Niles after a very long interrogation... Well, if you want to call it that. He pretty much told me everything he remembered. I got a lot of good stuff from him, and it's possible I can make a crack at it. I was wondering if you could help me from what you remember. You worked the original case, and I thought your expertise and guidance... I could really use it. I think Byron is innocent." "That's one hell of a story Allen. What do ya say... Why don't you meet me at the lake?"

"Meet you at the lake?"

"Yes... Meet me at the lake. You said expertise and guidance. I bet you haven't been at that lake in years. Hell, probably since it happened. You're working the case, and you gathered input. Get your ass on the location." Detective Wrighmas started to laugh.

"Okay, Darius. I can meet you there in forty five minutes, or so."

"That's perfect Allen. Be at the scene."

Darius hung up, followed by Detective Wrighmas. He exited out of the prison and entered to his car. He was then on his way to the murder scene at Lake Bodom. Detective Wrighmas began to laugh to himself. He knew that what Darius said, was right. He has not been at the lake in over forty years. This was his first time on location of the murder scene since it had happened. Detective Wrighmas even had a sense of being nervous, knowing that he was going back to 1 of the most horrific, murder scenes he has ever witnessed.

(On Location)

Detective Wrighmas was on location. He saw another vehicle parked and was able to know that Darius was already there waiting. After Detective Wrighmas exited out of his vehicle, he starred around. He felt uncomfortable being there. A short, heavyset man with a hat approached him. "Does anything look familiar to you Allen?"

"Yes, very familiar. It refreshes my memory to know that I am where one of histories unsolved murder took place." "Can you put anything together?"

"Tell me why we're really here Darius?"

"Me tell you?"

"Yes... You tell me."

"Do you have a memory flaw? Did you forget that you called me?"

"Not at all."

"Listen Allen, I come here every day. Every day since June 5, 1960. I walk these trails every day. You called and said the words expertise and guidance. If that's what you want then you won't question me. Is that understood?" "Absolutely."

"So I heard that the case got reopened, but I didn't know it was you that was working it." "Yeah they gave it to myself and some young buck, but I took it over. The kid doesn't know anything." They began to hike it down the trail.

"So, you got a piece of the guy?"

"I think I got more than a piece."

"That much, huh?"

"Yep. I had him for a little while. He spoke up and told me as much as he could remember, which a lot was. Good story, but I honestly believe it wasn't him. I even tried visualizing his story with him doing the killings. I just can't see it." "So that's the vibe you catch?"

"Yes. Do you think it could have been done by more than one party?"

"That's a good question. It could be that. If it were done by one party, the victims would have had to be incoherent." "I don't think I understand."

"They would have had to been asleep, or past out drunk."

"What about Byron, though?"

"What about him?"

"What do you think the chances were for him to survive and then after all these years he gets prosecuted?" "It's a unique happening. I will tell you there's a chance he did it. Just because he lived. But, Byron may have not been in the tent when it happened. He was found over the tent. He could have stepped out to take a piss, then ended up fighting somehow and so forth. Now, as for this trial and what not, do I think this does anything? Absolutely not.

They're just opening a new can of worms and screwing with this guy's life when he'll be found not guilty any way." "You sound so certain."

"I just know the legal system and all its bullshit flaws."

They stopped at an area where an X had been engraved in the ground.

"Do you know where we're at?" Darius asked.

"This is where it all took place."

"I want you to listen to me Allen."

"I'll listen to you man."

"This is where they pitched their tent. It wasn't the brightest spot to pitch a tent, but this is where they wanted it. Yeah it's on a slope, but again its where they wanted it." "Where are you going with all this, Darius?"

"You're main objective to me right now is to listen."

"I'm listening..."

"Then stop asking me why we are here, or where I am going with all this."

Darius began to explain more about the scene and what he remembered seeing.

"You know, the scene is imbedded in my mind... I know who killed them."

"You do?"

"Yeah. It was Val. He hated the youngsters, and he used to harass all of them."

"Do you really think he had it in him to do such a thing?"

"I think he had it in him."

"But what about Byron?"

"What about Byron?"

"You don't think there's any chance he did it?"

"I thought you said you believe in his innocence?"

"I do, but I'm trying to puzzle together how he became the fortunate one to survive, and we know his lover was killed the most brutal." "It's definite he put up some kind of fight. It's also possible that Val thought he was dead. What screws a lot of things up is we never recovered a weapon." "I know... There's not much we can do about that anymore."

"Here's one for you. Did you know that Byron and Seth's shoes were taken and hung up a couple hundred meters away from their site?" "I had not the slightest clue."

"Did you also know that people still complain about their shoes missing?"

"No!"

"People still camp here. People still come here all the time. It's very peaceful in the mornings here. What is strange to me is that the sun rose that day around three A.M. They were killed between four and six A.M." "So whoever it was, was pretty comfortable at the time setting."

"Here's another did you know... Did you know the kids on the bicycles stated they saw a man near the scene when they saw the drunken man?" "Where did you get that information?"

"I was the detective then."

"Did you figure out who it was?"

"He's an unknown man, but it doesn't mean it was him. There were other campers that night. A women washing clothes in the lake saw them swimming. Why they would want to swim in freezing water is beyond me, but then to pitch a tent on a slope is beyond me too. There was some fisherman here that night as well." "Did you figure out if Byron, or Seth got into an argument or anything like that?"

"That's something you should already know. Did you go over, or look at the other suspects?" "I did."

"Does anyone of them stand out to you in particular?"

"Hansman did at first, but..."

"He was in the hospital hours before their deaths. I know who killed them. It was Val. Did you know he confessed to the murders?" "Yeah I know that."

"Did you know he confessed it four times?"

"Not four times, no."

"He confessed to the murders four times and then he did himself in. He drowned himself right here in the lake." "But you investigated that. There was no way he could have done it. Isn't that right?"

"Yes. His wife did give him an alibi, but it turned out that her life was threatened by him if she spoke up and she admitted that on her deathbed." Detective Wrighmas stood silent and just stared into Darius.

"Well I'll be damned."

"Val Karstrom killed those kids. He's the one who did it. There were a couple of confessions heard from the people under suspicion, but all whacked themselves out later on down the line. Look how many suspects we had and look at the count of suicides. The one mystery that stands out would be the unknown man who was seen near the tent." "Byron told me about a man they all saw. He was by himself. They saw him one time. The guy even talked to Seth and Angel. They didn't get a name, or anything." "So there's one man with no established identity and the rest of our suspects are dead, or have concrete alibis. There's one man left, which is a victim of three murders. The case went nowhere forty years ago, and it's going to go nowhere forty years later." "I have to say, you opened my mind a lot more and have given me a lot to think about."

"Well I'm glad I didn't waste my time with you. Now that you have my input, do you want to know what I think went down here, that night to early morning on June fifth?" "Thrill me Darius."

(Past Time- 1960)

The companions all rested in the tent. With the boys on each end and both girls laying in the middle, they were all making out. It was quiet besides of the sounds being made from their wet, sloppy kissing. The fire was almost out. It was beginning to die off from it no longer being occupied. There for, there was no lighting on their site anymore . It was now just pitch dark. With the 4 lovers being preoccupied with their making out and other activities, they were not able to detect the sound of footsteps as if someone was coming, or if there was an animal approaching. The sounds of sticks snapping and leaves cracking grew louder and closer to their camping site. Suddenly Seth was able to hear the sounds. He immediately stopped in the middle of what he was doing and sat up. "Do you guys hear that?" He asked in a low whisper.

"Yeah I hear that. Sounds like someone's coming." Amelia said, whispering back.

"It might just be an animal." Whispered Byron.

"That's a pretty big animal." Whispered Seth.

All of a sudden, from out of the blue, their tent began to get attacked. It was being thrashed at with a blade that was slicing holes through it. The companions began to panic. The girls were screaming hysterically while both Byron and Seth were aiding them with their protection. "What the fuck is going on!" Yelled Seth, at the top of his lungs.

Byron began an attempt to escape the tent, but it then collapsed on them, followed by the blade entering and exiting out of Seth's back. He screamed in anguish as the blade entered and exited him several more times. At this point in time, Byron was still trying to escape from the tent, both the girls were still screaming, and Seth lay over Angel as he continued to be stabbed to death. "What do you want? Please stop!" Screamed Byron.

Byron then was struck down on the head with an object, almost knocking him unconscious. It split the top of his head

open, and he started to bleed. At the
second he finally came to, he saw his point
of escape. He crawled out of a hole made
from a knife thrash. He just ripped at the
hole and made it wide enough for him to
crawl out of. As he reached the outside, he
could not see much around him from it being
too dark. He lay on his stomach with his
head injury trying to make it to his feet.
In that moment, he could only hear 1 voice
screaming and crying. He could also hear
the sound of someone else being hurt. He
heard a gurgling sound coming from the
collapsed tent along with a throw down
noise. He finally reached his feet but
could not keep his balance. At first he
staggered a bit. It took a short moment for
him to reach the control of his legs. When
he finally could, he came to see a shadowed
figure, raining down on the tent with a
sharp, pointed object. Angel was still
trapped in the collapsed tent, with Seth's
now stabbed and abused corpse, holding her
down. She screamed the sound of horror.
Amelia lay next to her being, being stabbed
and gruesomely mutilated. Amelia was
already dead, but the reaper continued to

stab her repeatedly. Byron could not do anything at first being that he was fighting himself to recover from a bash on the head. When he could clearly see what was happening around him it was too late. "Stop!" Byron screamed as loud as he could.

As soon as he attempted to run to their aid, he was immediately struck once again only this time across the face with the blunt object. This sent Byron to the ground unconscious, with a broken jaw. He landed hard with dead weight. He was unconscious before he hit the ground. He did not flinch a single joint, or muscle. That is when he began to be stabbed. After being stabbed a number of times. It was sudden when Angel began screaming louder for help. She was half way out of the tent when she saw Byron being savagely attacked. Angel was the only 1 alive inside the collapsed tent. It was not much of a tent anymore. What was left of the tent was absolutely nothing more than a tarnished, ripped, blood drenched fabric that carried 2 battered corpses and a helpless woman who was trapped under her dead lovers corpse.

Once she finally managed to crawl half way
out, she continued to scream as loud as she
could until she finally gave up her ghost.
All she could do was lay their helpless.
Being that her legs were still stuck under
her lover's corpse, she could only watch
the reaper move toward her. Once the reaper
settled in, the horrific sounds of
screaming for help erupted. Angel began to
get slashed open repeatedly, a countless
number of times. There was not a single
thing she could do. She could not help
herself. The position she turned up in was
terrifying just itself. With her legs being
trapped and held down under a corpse, as
well as being stuck inside of a collapsed
tent and being continuously stabbed until
her body expired surcease.

(Present Time- 2004)

    "That's what your theory is?"
Detective Wrighmas asked, with a sound of
doubt in his voice. "That's is my theory,
and from the sound of it, you have doubts."

"Yeah Darius I do have some minor doubts, but that doesn't mean that you're wrong."

"Where are you getting at Allen?"

"So you say that Byron managed to escape the tent, but to be bludgeoned in the head and stabbed several times?" "That's in my theory, yes. It's also where his helpless body would lay on the ground, bleeding out with a broken jaw along with the lacerations to his head." "Are you also saying that Seth was the first one to be dead among Angel and Amelia?"

"Right. He was the first to go. He was stabbed to death in his back and body. He never left the tent. Which would lead to Amelia and Angel, who was also stabbed to death all over her body? The only differentiation was that she had gashes. Seth didn't." "So Seth and Angel died similar deaths except for the gashes?"

"Exactly. Keep in mind that they were all bludgeoned by the same object. That leaves Byron alive, but with the same wounds." "That would only leave Amelia being the only one who was gruesomely attacked and mutilated. She was still being stabbed even after she was dead... But why? "Why is a good question. It can also tell us that there was a good possibility that she was the last to go. Could also be the first." "I'm losing you Darius."

"If she was the first to go, that means the killer came in, striking the tent, and she was in the midst of the weapon the whole time. That's not what happened. She was the last to go because being that he was already in the heat up passion, he got a bit carried away and kept going until he got tired. Only to find out that 2 parties were still alive, which leads to the gashes on Angel." "And why Byron alive? He suffered many wounds and a broken jaw, and he was fortunate enough to survive the savage attack." "He didn't know Angel was still alive so by the time he was killing Byron, he found out that Angel wasn't dead. He slices her up, Byron doesn't move, and the killer thinks he's dead." "I like your theory, but minds a bit different."

"Let's hear it."

"These are facts from Byron himself...
The girls were already asleep in the tent.
Him and Seth were still drinking at the
fire. Seth gets up to take a piss, and
that's all he can remember. We established
that they were the first to be attacked."
"You got all that huh?"

"Yes I do, but I do like how you said,
Amelia was the last to go. I also liked how
you compared the wounds." "Here's the
golden question, and it could also answer
your brief theory of Byron Niles being the
culprit murderer. So I hope you have a
golden answer." "I hope I do."

"Take my theory and now put your facts
in the mix of the time they retired to the
tent. Think of the similar wounds they all
had, but despite Amelia. Don't give me a
reliable answer. All you have to do is tell
me if you understand my point of
direction... Now do you understand?"
"Darius I understand your point of
direction crystal clear. I have to say,
thank you for your help. You definitely put

a part of my brain to rest except for one thing? "What one thing would that be?"

"We may subconsciously know who it was, but in reality we'll never know. It will always be an unsolved murder mystery." "It was over forty years ago, and we should leave it be. We may never know who really done it. The way to look at it is that life is the stage before your spirit is called home to the afterlife. That was there calling to come home. As for Byron, it wasn't his time to go home." "That's a very positive outlook on it."

"You can see it as an outlook, but I accepted it as that being what it is. It may not have been an easy way to pass, but they are home now and they have their peace."

(Trial Year and Outcome- 2005)

Byron Niles was put on trial for the murder of his 2 friends Seth Hegg, Angel Copolas and his lover Amelia Borger at Lake

Bodom in June, 1960. 44 years later they brought him up on the murder charges with new forensic evidence that could lead to his guilt for the murders. Byron stated in court that he had no memory of what happened. He recalls kissing his lover for a final good night and then to waking in a hospital, figuring that he wrecked on his motorcycle. The prosecution stated a case against Byron that he collapsed the tent so he could easily murder the 3 of them. The wounds on Byron were self-inflicted, and he lay over the tent, making it look like the murders were done by another party. This would all be over his jealous anger towards his lover. However, his defense argued that he had no reason to harm his lover or his friends. They also stated that his wounds were similar and could not have been inflicted by self-harm. The murders would have had to been acted out by 2 or more parties. The defense felt that the scene was taken down much too early, and the investigated work was done too fast and that the investigative team did not do a thorough investigation. The prosecution was calling for a life sentence to Byron Niles.

They stated that his wounds to his face and head would not have made him unconscious and there for question how he managed to survive such a savage attack, comparing injuries on the 3 victims. They also questioned why he did not go for help and also presented that there was no DNA from any outside assailant. Byron's defense still argued that the murders had to been completed by 2 or more persons. Byron still stated that with his injuries, he was completely not capable of committing such acts, especially against his 2 friends and lover. After the long term trial, Byron Niles was acquitted of all charges. There was no evidence that could prove Byron guilty of the 3 murders. He was formally granted $60,000 for his time he spent in prison and for the mental stability he suffered on such accusations brought against him and the minimal time he was incarcerated.

(Byron Niles)

Byron Niles worked in community
transportation. After a long term of
healing over the event that took place in
1960, he lived a regular working class
life. Although he never fully recovered
mentally from the day in June of 1960. It
only got worse for him after 40 years have
passed. The 40 years of silence was broken
when the FNBI reopened the case against
him. They reopened it with new forensic
evidence which never proved a thing. It
only caused him to endure mental anguish
all over again. Byron Niles is alive today,
and he is in his early 70s. He is the sole
survivor of the Lake Bodom blood murders
who was charged and found not guilty of the
3 murders in 2005.

(Point of Views)

Despite the Lake Bodom blood murders
still being a highly talked about unsolved

murder in the Finnish land. What about in America? Or everywhere else, all over the world. For those who are familiar with the unsolved murder, or for those who remember the happening taking place, ask yourself what really happened? From the list of numerous suspects, did 1 of them manage to slip out of the reach of justice? Were they all truly innocent? Was it really the unidentified man, or did Byron really get away with those gruesome murders. It is the not knowing that really eats at your brain. A lot may look over the story and facts of the Lake Bodom blood murders and right away point their finger at Byron Niles just because he survived. Every pin point aspect against Byron can lead to his guilt, but the point is that he was found not guilty. 2 suspects from the list committed suicide after confessing the murders, but 1 in particular stood out and that was Val Karstrom. Val was a man with 4 confessions and a wife who stated she protected him by giving an alibi. It is in the facts that he would have killed her if she did not protect him, just to charge Byron 40 some years later. In such a case, you can have a

Byron Vs. Val case. This book was written
based off true, researched facts. There is
a handful of murder scenarios. 1 is even
portrayed as Byron Niles being the culprit.
1 other is based off of what you can read
from the facts and research and the first
murder scenario from what you read is just
the simple point of what this real life
story is about. The point is nobody will
ever know precisely what happened on that
heartbroken, early morning on June 5, 1960.
There is 1 person in the entire world that
can tell you everything that happened on
that day, but what you read in your
research and what you read in this book, in
the end is all left up to you. You are not
expected to believe any of the murder
scenarios in this story. Again the murder
scenarios were based from 1, the storyline.
2, Byron's charges against him and 3, what
was gathered from the facts of the case.
These are strictly on the murder scenarios.
As for the story mode itself, we don't know
everything they did the night before, and
we don't know what the interrogation was
really all about. This is a simple story
written based from the murders and the

murder scenarios are the main focus point.
Once again, there is 1 person in the entire
world who really knows what happened that
night and early morning. Everything you
come across in research will all be up to
what you think. This is a strong versus
between opinions and perspectives. In a
case like this, you cannot have a
perspective on these facts. It is all
opinionated due to the fact that it is a
murder unsolved. Here are some of the
concrete facts.

Byron Niles was the only person alive
and outside of the tent. He sustained minor
injuries compared to the 3 murdered. His
lover was found mutilated and killed more
savagely opposed to the 2 others. Out of
opinion a lot of people would agree that he
is guilty, but what about Val Karstrom? Val
Karstrom was known to be a tempered man,
who hated the young campers. His kiosk
stand was not far from their campsite. He
was known to confess the murders 4 times
and even drowned himself in the lake. He
had a concrete alibi from his wife that he
was home that night and morning. His wife

admits she covered for him, and he threatened to kill her if she spoke the truth. She admitted that on her deathbed. Those are all 100% facts. Now ask yourself, why reopen the case 44 years later when it was obvious that Val Karstrom was the Lake Bodom murderer. The defense would be hearsay. So again, it is all left up to YOU to believe what happened on June 5, 1960.

I, Matt Demas did not write this story to offend any party what so ever. I didn't write it claiming to be an expert either and I'm not. There's a band named Children of Bodom. I've enjoyed listening to them for some years now. I never knew what their name meant until a close friend of mine told me a brief story about it. I couldn't believe I never knew it.

I actually researched it one day and read on it. I thought it was a creepy story. Then to know that it actually happened, I grieved over it. I thought to myself why haven't they ever wrote a book, or make a movie from it? In America at least and I'm not talking about the reporters' books written in the past. I learned that it's still a popular subject in the Finnish land, so I don't know if there are films written there. I thought that the Lake Bodom murders would also be a popular topic in my particular field and even as far as the film industry. So I decided to write a story on the Lake Bodom murders. I wanted to bring it out and share it with all my fellow independent writers like myself and filmmakers. We do know the band Children of Bodom, but ask yourself, how many of you knew the real story? An event like this should not be forgotten.

I read a brief story on the murders that took place. I then gathered as much research on the Lake Bodom murders as I could and believe me I didn't stop. I will tell you that I wrote this story based off a lot of facts. However I will tell you even though it's somewhat common sense. We all don't know what the victims were doing at the lake on the eve of their deaths. We couldn't tell you everything they did, and we don't know exactly how each death was dealt out. So when you read the story, please keep in mind that it's a story based off a real event. We know the real primary story. So you get the story of four campers at Lake Bodom who are having a joyful time, prior to what we already know is going to happen.

Being that the Lake Bodom murders are an unsolved murder case, and the survivor was charged and found not guilty, I started with interrogation scenes. We all know he was interrogated after he was brought to arrest. We don't really know what happened in the interrogation room. So keep in mind that you're just reading a story based off the real life event. I even added in different murder scenarios. I had to keep one basic scenario for the story itself. I also added in a scenario as "Byron" being the murderer just for the fact that he was a suspect. With all the murder scenarios, I added in the facts of how they were murdered and tried to be as specific as the facts stated. I also added a scenario based from my own opinion, which I'm sure you'll have by now. When I wrote this story I knew in the end that it would come down to one thing and in the end, it's really what you think happened.

www.ingramcontent.com/pod-product-compliance
Lightning Source LLC
Chambersburg PA
CBHW051725040426

42447CB00008B/984